CONTENTS

GN00739312

CONTENTS

KEY:

DLR = Nearest Docklands Light Railway Station

⊖ = Nearest London Transport Underground Station

⇌ = Nearest British Rail Station

🅿 = Car Parking (for locations see page 46)

🚌 = Coach Parking

♿ = Access for disabled visitors

✗ = Refreshment facilities available

[CD] = Age limit for child discount

➊ = Member of the LTB

1

Children's London, now in its second edition, is written for parents and children who want to make the most of what London has to offer. In this second edition we have added new attractions and deleted a few that have moved away. We have also introduced some new ideas into our editorial section which we hope will stimulate those already familiar with London and those who have come here for the first time.

The attractions list is a comprehensive guide to places which children of different ages will enjoy. There are suggestions on how they can be combined with other nearby attractions.

We have looked in greater detail on eating out with children as this can sometimes seem a problem.

In the getting around section there is information on special tickets and discounts. Families travelling to London from other parts of Britain should also look closely at week-end break packages offered by tour operators and hotels. These often include discounts and free admission to some attractions as well as Travel-cards.

We hope that you will enjoy this book and London.

The Editor

Most children love to ride on top of one of the capital's famous double decker buses. They offer an excellent view of London and riding high above the crowds is one of the most enjoyable ways to travel. However, the best way to beat central London's traffic congestion is to take the "tube" or Underground as most of the main attractions have a station nearby. London Regional Transport offers a selection of travel tickets to help you get around. Children under 5 travel free and those under 14 travel at reduced rates. 14 and 15 year olds can travel at child rates if they carry a child rate photocard – available from post offices on production of a passport-sized photograph and proof of age.

DISCOUNT TICKETS

The *Travelcard* allows freedom of travel on the bus and Underground network in whichever zones you choose, for one or seven days. When buying a seven day Travelcard, you must also bring a passport-sized photograph. The tickets are available from any Underground station. Further information from London Transport Travel Information Centres (for addresses and opening times see TRAVEL INFORMATION section). Overseas visitors to London can purchase the Visitor's Travelcard overseas through tour operators and travel agents. This is available for one, three, four and seven days (off-peak) and includes discount vouchers for tourist attractions.

The *Capitalcard* is valid for bus, Underground and rail travel for one or seven days (passport-sized photograph required for the seven day ticket) and they can be purchased from any Underground or British Rail station.

For unlimited travel on all London Transport buses, for outer and inner zones, buy a *One Day Bus Pass* available from most outer London Underground stations, bus garages and newsagents.

TRAVEL INFORMATION

LONDON REGIONAL TRANSPORT
55 Broadway, London SW1
Tel: 01-222 1234 – All enquiries 24-hour service, seven days per week.
LRT operates a number of Travel Information Centres in the following Underground stations which are open to personal callers:
Euston – Mon–Sat 07.15–18.00 (19.30 Fri), Sun 08.15–18.00
King's Cross – Mon–Thurs and Sun 08.15–18.00, Fri 07.15–19.30, Sat 07.15–18.00
Oxford Circus – Mon–Sat 08.15–18.00
Piccadilly Circus – Daily 08.15–21.30
St. James's Park – Mon–Fri 08.15–18.00
Victoria – Daily 08.15–21.30

AND AT HEATHROW AIRPORT:
Terminals 1, 2, 3 station –
Mon–Sat 07.15–18.30, Sun 08.15–18.30
Terminal 1 Arrivals –
Mon–Sat 07.15–22.15 (21.00 Sat), Sun 08.15–22.00
Terminal 2 Arrivals –
Mon–Sat 07.15–21.00, Sun 08.15–22.00
Terminal 3 Arrivals –
Mon–Sat 06.30–13.15, Sun 08.15–15.00
Terminal 4 Arrivals –
Mon–Sat 06.30–18.30, Sun 08.15–18.30

BRITISH RAIL
BR Travel Centres provide comprehensive information on
British Rail services/holidays etc. to personal callers.
Travel Centres at principal BR stations:
Cannon Street – Mon–Fri 08.00–18.30
Charing Cross – Daily 08.00–19.30
Euston – Mon–Sat 07.00–23.30, Sun 08.00–23.30
King's Cross – Daily 07.00–23.00
London Bridge – Mon–Fri 08.00–18.30, Sat 08.30–14.00
Paddington – Mon–Sat 08.00–20.30, Sun 09.00–17.00
St. Pancras – Mon–Sat 07.30–21.00, Sun 07.45–21.00
Victoria – Daily 07.15–21.15
Waterloo – Mon–Sat 08.00–21.00, Sun 09.00–21.00

SIGHTSEEING
COACH TOURS
If your time is limited or it is your first time in London, why
not take advantage of one of the excellent non-stop
panoramic tours on offer, such as the London Transport
Original Sightseeing Tour. Most follow a twenty mile route
which passes all the famous sights and attractions.
Cityrama's "talking buses" are equipped with taped
commentary in eight languages. Culture Bus follow a route
with over twenty carefully chosen stops which allow you to
hop on and off and sightsee without a guide at your own
pace. Most of the established tour companies also run full
and half-day tours which take you inside Westminster
Abbey, the Tower of London and St. Paul's Cathedral, with
a registered Blue Badge guide to add interest to your visit.
Contact the following LTB members for panoramic and
sightseeing tours:
London Regional Transport: 01-222 1234.
Cityrama: 01-720 6663.
CultureBus: Southend (0702) 355711.
Harrods Sightseeing: 01-581 3603.
London Pride: Purfleet (0708) 865656/865201.
London Tour Company: 01-734 3502.
Evan Evans: 01-930 2377.
Frames Rickards: 01-837 3111.

DRIVER GUIDES

You may also take a guided tour with a Driver Guide. They are all qualified; some are cab-drivers who have become Blue Badge Guides and will give individual tours for up to four people. The following are LTB members:
British Tours Ltd: 01-629 5267.
Driver Guides Association: 01-839 2498.
Go-by-Guide Ltd: 01-350 2408.

GUIDED WALKING TOURS

Many children come to London as part of a school project or for educational purposes. You may find that a guided walking tour is the perfect way to bring a subject to life. Tours usually begin at a centrally located tube station and last for approximately two hours. Tours include historically based walks; literary themes such as "A Journey Through Dickens' London"; "legal" walks – "Inside the Law Courts", and even blood-curdling tours of plague ridden London! See listings magazines for full details or call one of the LTB member companies listed below.
City Walks: 01-278 3720.
Cockney Walks: 01-504 9159.
Citisights: 01-739 2372.
Discovering London: Brentwood (0277) 213704.
Footloose in London: 01-435 0259.
London Suburban Tours: 01-550 5587.
London Walks: 01-882 2763.
Streets of London: 01-882 3414.

WATERWAYS

RIVER TRIPS

Why not explore London from the famous River Thames? Greenwich, rich in maritime history, and the Tower of London, one of London's most ancient landmarks, are popular destinations.

There are daily services running approximately every 20 minutes from Westminster Pier (journey time just 30 minutes) or every 30 minutes from Charing Cross Pier (journey time 20 minutes) to Tower Pier.

Beyond the Tower, downriver, lies Greenwich. Boats leave every 30 minutes from Westminster, Charing Cross and Tower Piers to Greenwich (journey time 45 minutes from Westminster Pier or 30 minutes from Tower Pier).

Beyond Greenwich lies the giant Thames Barrier, London's protection against flooding. A boat service to the Barrier, landing at the Visitor Centre, operates from Westminster Pier generally at 75 minute intervals during the summer months (reduced service in winter, journey time 1½ hours). There is a summer service from Greenwich Pier.

In the other direction, it is possible to reach Kew Gardens, Richmond and Hampton Court. Boat services operate during the summer months from Westminster Pier, to Kew every 30 minutes (journey time 1½ hours each way). There are four boats daily to Richmond and Hampton Court (journey time 2½ and 3-4 hours respectively). Times vary.

Informal commentaries are given on boat services at the discretion of the crew. Snacks and a bar service are available on most boats except the 20-minute Westminster to Tower summer service.

Riverboat Information Service: 01-730 4812.

CANAL TRIPS

It is possible to explore the "backwaters" of north London by taking a trip along the Regent's Canal, which was opened in 1820. Canal trips run daily during the summer months and at weekends in winter from Little Venice, London Zoo and Camden Lock. From Little Venice (nearest underground – Warwick Avenue), where the Regent and Grand Union Canals meet, you'll see the elegant houses designed by Nash. You may like to get off at the London Zoo landing stage, to visit the animals, or continue the trip (journey time 1 hour) to Camden Lock – an attractive area of renovated Victorian warehouses now containing craft workshops. From Camden Lock you can travel to Limehouse through 12 locks on a London Waterbus tour.

For further information on the Canal Boat services, contact one of the following LTB member companies:
London Waterbus Company: 01-482 2550
Jason's Trip: 01-286 3428

THE HISTORY AND TRADITIONS OF LONDON

Start your exploration of London's past at the Museum of London. Here the displays are arranged chronologically and new material is added as archaeological excavations in the City bring in new finds.

One of the most dramatic displays is of the Great Fire of London and, not far away at Tower Hill, you can visit All Hallows by the Tower, the church from which Samuel Pepys watched the progress of the fire.

This is close to the Tower of London which of course emerged unscathed from the Great Fire. The White Tower was the first stone building of its size in London put up by William the Conqueror. The Romans a few centuries before had surrounded the city with a stone wall. You can follow the outline of this wall, using the London Wall Walk map from the Museum of London. Remains are clearly shown. You can also find out more about Roman London and later periods by joining a guided walk from the Museum of London. Contact Citisights, see p. 5.

Some of London's smaller museums give interesting insights in local history. At the Geffrye Museum in East London there are room settings showing how people lived over five centuries. The Passmore Edwards Museum at Stratford and the Bruce Castle Museum at Tottenham are just two well worth exploring. More information on museums throughout London in LTB's guides "Exploring Outer London" and "Exploring Central London".

London's past is relived through its traditions and ceremonies. The Changing the Guard at Buckingham Palace is how the Sovereign was ensured of protection; at the Tower of London the Ceremony of the Keys has taken place for 700 years and ensures that those who lock the gates are both safe and do the job properly. You can get tickets by writing well in advance to The Resident Governor, Queen's House, HM Tower of London, London EC3.

The Lord Mayor's Show (first Saturday of November) brings both colourful floats and traditional uniforms to the streets of the City, as the new Lord Mayor rides in the Gold Coach to the Law Courts to be sworn in.

The Queen's carriages, kept at the Royal Mews, come out for Trooping the Colour in June, and for the State Opening of Parliament (usually) in early November, as well as for royal weddings. Visiting Heads of State are usually welcomed at Victoria Station and drive through Westminster in procession to Buckingham Palace in one of the state coaches.

There is more information on traditions and ceremonies in LTB's book "Traditional London", see inside back cover. For official state visits, check the daily papers.

Any exploration of Britain's scientific past – and some of its future – must start at the Science Museum. From the earliest machines including steam railway engines to advanced space travel; from crude versions of surgical instruments to lasers; the Museum has something to show. Launch Pad – the Interactive Technology Centre has over 100 computer exhibits for children to learn from.

The early days of air transport can also be explored at the Royal Air Force Museum, while the beginnings of sea travel are on display at the National Maritime Museum. In both museums there are interesting historic tableaux and displays bringing the technology to the present day. While in Greenwich, a visit to the Old Royal Observatory reveals the earliest time-pieces and the development of the computer clock. Not far away is the massive Thames Barrier, designed to hold back the River Thames in full flood. The visitor centre illustrates dramatically what could have happened before the Barrier was built.

Thames Barrier

While in this part of London, cross the Thames (the free Woolwich Ferry is still going – until a new bridge is built a little further downstream) and take a look at North Woolwich Old Station Museum showing the history of the Great Eastern Railway.

Close by are the Royal Docks where a massive redevelopment programme is underway. Already a new airport, the London City Airport, has opened, used by Short Take-Off and Landing Aircraft. In the Isle of Dogs try out the new Docklands Light Railway using driver-less, computer managed trains, on tracks which in some cases run dramatically above the old Docks.

The Museum of London has already collected some of the old docks machinery and memorabilia to form the basis for a Museum of Docklands, due to open in the Royal Docks some time in 1988. Here and in the Isle of Dogs the huge Satellite Discs of Mercury and British Telecom receive and send television broadcasts and other communications. Underground optic fibre cables carry millions of units of information for the financial industry.

Up until now, London's financial centre has been firmly in the City of London. But Docklands is proving attractive for banks and trading organisations. Already the London Futures & Options Exchange is installed in St. Katharine Docks. The Big Bang in 1986 has changed the nature of the Trading Floor at the London Stock Exchange. The visitors' gallery now has a new presentation explaining what is happening in the age of computer dealing. Lloyd's visitors' gallery overlooks a trading floor on four levels where pieces of paper still dominate. There is an interesting exhibition of the history of insurance and an exciting ride in an outside lift to get to the Fourth Floor level.

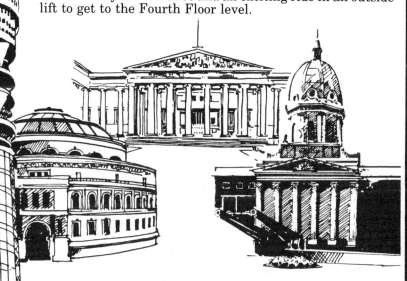

The Telecom Technology Showcase in Queen Victoria Street gives an introduction to more advanced ways of communicating while looking at the history of the telephone. The Telecom Tower, the former Post Office Tower, is still closed to visitors.

Holography, the art of three-dimensional photography is on view at two Light Fantastic galleries – in Covent Garden and in the Trocadero. Nearby in the Trocadero is the Guinness World of Records, where computers are used to illustrate some world-breaking records.

Advances made in film and television will go on show at a new Museum of Moving Image now under construction on London's South Bank, next to the National Film Theatre. It will open in June 1988. And at the rebuilt Alexandra Palace, where the BBC made their first television broadcast, a television museum is being created out of the old studios and will open in 1989.

And at the London Transport Museum in Covent Garden, the original Shillibeer omnibus – horse-drawn, of course – is to be found close to the latest in tube train design.

Those with an interest in science and technology are spoilt for choice in London.

SIGHTSEEING WITH CHILDREN OF DIFFERENT AGES AND THE UNDER 5's

Visiting London with small children needs a little extra planning. A large, busy city is not always the most accommodating place for people with prams and slow-walking small children. So the first rule is to take a folding pushchair or carrying frame for small children and, if appropriate, a harness for walking children, who might stray.

If you are going to a crowded event or attraction, it is sensible to ensure that young children unable to speak clearly for themselves, and non-English speaking children, have a note on them of their name and address (of the hotel, if you are a visitor to London), should you become separated.

Plan your travel carefully avoiding the main commuter rush hours if you are going by public transport, and find out about parking facilities before you set out if you are using a car. There are travel discounts for children, see p. 3, and most children will enjoy a panoramic sightseeing tour with a view of London from the top-deck. A river-trip is also a good way of seeing London and keeping everyone together.

The programme of sightseeing should obviously be geared to each child's interest. This can be difficult if they are of different ages and may mean splitting children up, so older children can get on with the computer games in the Science Museum while younger children run around in Kensington Gardens.

Make sure that you give clear instructions where to meet up again, and have a fall-back should you not find each other. Older children should have enough money for a phone-call or their fare home, and should be given sensible advice on whom to ask for help, e.g. a museum official or police.

Don't try to cram too much into one day, and allow for plenty of breaks for drinks, toilet-visits etc. Museums, galleries and tourist attractions are well equipped with toilet facilities; the larger stores and railway stations have Mother and Baby facilities. Underground stations are usually without any toilets at all. Restaurants all provide toilet facilities but this is not the case with small cafes. Public lavatories are widely available and the new free-standing toilets cost 10p. In larger public lavatories, children should be accompanied.

Where to eat should also be planned. If you decide to bring your own picnic, the parks are welcoming. Some museums also provide indoor picnic facilities, should it rain. Fast-food restaurants of every type can be found throughout London and these are enjoyed by most children. See the eating out section on p. 47. One American restaurant will look after children while their parent(s) do some shopping or sightseeing on their own!

Pubs in central London have no children's rooms on the whole, and remember that licensing restrictions mean that most winebars cannot serve children. If you succumb to demands for ice-creams and soft drinks, check the prices carefully before you buy, particularly from ice-cream stalls or vans.

Film and theatre shows are plentiful to be enjoyed by children with or without adults. There are those geared specifically to children, and there are a variety of plays and musicals in London's West End which older children will also enjoy. A publication such as *What's On Where to Go*, or the *Independent* newspaper, carries descriptions of current West End productions.

The National Theatre and the Barbican Centre have back-stage tours, foyer entertainment and buffets as well as exhibitions in a comfortable environment, where those not watching a play can wait.

With a little planning and forethought an outing in London with children of different ages can be a real pleasure.

LONDON WITH THE UNDER 5s

The numerous crowded pavements, stairs, escalators and revolving doors in the capital, makes sightseeing with a pram a pretty awkward operation. Less cumbersome is a folding pushchair or carrying frame. If you don't happen to have a pushchair with you, you may like to hire one (see addresses below).

HIRE EQUIPMENT

Chelsea Baby Hire
52 Glebe Place, SW3
Tel: 01-351 3688

As well as pushchairs here you can hire cots, highchairs, strollers and car seats. Delivery and collection service.

Abracadabra Baby Hire, Contact:
Elizabeth Baxter
Tel: East Horsley (04865) 5142
or:
Bridget Hughes
Tel: Dorking (0306) 882242

Delivery and collection service.

MOTHER AND BABY FACILITIES

Shops

Most of the large department stores in London are well equipped to deal with families. Below is a list of some of those providing facilities for feeding and/or changing babies. Of particular interest are the facilities provided by John Lewis and Mothercare, both in Oxford Street, which fathers are also welcome to use. A most thoughtful and useful innovation.

Brent Cross Shopping Centre, NW4
Tel: 01-202 8095

⊖ Brent Cross

Facilities on upper ground floor adjacent to Ladies.

BhS
252 Oxford Street, W1
Tel: 01-629 2011

⊖ Oxford Circus

Mother and Baby Rooms adjacent to "Patio" restaurant 1st floor.

Debenhams Department Store
Oxford Street, W1
Tel: 01-580 3000

⊖ Oxford Circus/Bond Street

Ladies toilets 3rd floor.

continued overleaf

House of Fraser
318 Oxford Street, W1
Tel: 01-629 8800

⊖ Oxford Circus

Mothers' Room 2nd floor.

Fortnum and Mason
181 Piccadilly, W1
Tel: 01-734 8040

⊖ Green Park/Piccadilly Circus

Spacious ladies room 1st floor.

Hamley's (Toy Store)
188-196 Regent Street, W1
Tel: 01-734 3161

⊖ Oxford Circus

Ladies on 4th floor.

Harrods
Knightsbridge, SW1
Tel: 01-730 1234

⊖ Knightsbridge

Mother and Baby Room in Ladies 4th floor, more facilities in "Children's Shop" 1st floor.

Heal's
196 Tottenham Court Road, W1
Tel: 01-636 1666

⊖ Goodge Street

Ladies on 1st floor with changing area.

John Lewis
Oxford Street, W1
Tel: 01-629 7711

⊖ Oxford Circus

Baby changing room on 4th floor. For mother and fathers.

Mothercare
461 Oxford Street, W1
Tel: 01-629 6621

⊖ Marble Arch

Mothers Room with facilities for nursing mothers and baby changing. Fathers welcome. (Similar facilities available at two other central London branches, at 164 Oxford Street and Brompton Road, Knightsbridge with more stores to follow).

Peter Jones
Sloane Square, SW1
Tel: 01-730 3434

⊖ Sloane Square

Mother and baby room 3rd floor.

Selfridges
Oxford Street, W1
Tel: 01-629 1234

⊖ Bond Street

Ladies toilets on 3rd floor.

BRITISH RAIL STATIONS

Euston
Nursing room in Ladies opposite platforms 2/3.

King's Cross
Nursing room in Ladies on platform 8.

Liverpool Street
Nursing rooms in Ladies opposite platforms 14/15.

Paddington
Nursing room in First Aid room by platform 1 (not open 24 hours).

St. Pancras
Nursing mothers may use ladies waiting room next to ladies toilets alongside platform 7.

Victoria
Ladies by platform 15 (close to Grosvenor Hotel entrance) has baby changing facilities on 1st floor.

Waterloo
Ladies toilets opposite platform 16. (Ring bell by disabled WCs to gain access to mother and baby room.)

TOY SHOPS

Hamley's
188-196 Regent Street, W1
Tel: 01-734 3161

⊖ Oxford Circus

5 floors of games and toys, the largest toy shop in the world.

Toys R Us
78-80 High Street, N22
Tel: 01-881 6636/7

⊖ Wood Green

Huge toy warehouse.

Early Learning Centre
225 Kensington High Street, W8
Tel: 01-937 0419

⊖ High Street Kensington

One of a chain of shops specialising in books, games and toys for children up to eight years old. Each shop has an area where children can play under parental supervision.

And for the toy victims of over boisterous children!

The Dolls Hospital
16 Dawes Road, SW6
Tel: 01-385 2081

⊖ Fulham Broadway

A casualty ward for dolls and teddies.

CRÈCHES

Permanent professional playcare facilities are available to travellers using Heathrow and Luton airports and there are plans for a centre to open at Gatwick in 1988. In addition to this, many major London exhibitions and shows make space available for children to play in, leaving parents free to visit exhibition stands.

Volvo Playcare Centre
Departure Lounge, Heathrow
Airport Terminal 4,
Heathrow, Middx.

Free service catering for up to 35 children between the ages of 2 and 8 years and staffed by qualified nursery nurses.

Open: Mon–Sat 07.00–22.00, Sun 08.00–21.00.

Vauxhall World of Children
Departure Lounge, Luton Airport,
Luton, Beds.

Open: Daily 06.00–22.00

For further information on the above centres, please contact: **World of Children: High Wycombe (0494) 25051.**

While you're sightseeing take advantage of discounts on admission. Most attractions offer 50% discount for children under the age of 14, 15 or 16.

If you are a visitor from abroad then you may be interested in an *Open To View* ticket. This ticket offers unlimited entry to over 550 properties around Great Britain and is valid for one month. The Tower of London and Hampton Court are among the properties you may visit.

It is possible to buy yearly or life membership of the English Heritage organisation and have free entry to these famous monuments. The National Trust, who also have yearly or life membership subscription schemes, have some properties in the London area.

Don't hesitate to contact the London Tourist Board for further information or advice.

English Heritage tickets available from:
English Heritage Membership Department, P.O. Box 43, Ruislip, Middx. HA4 0XW.

National Trust Membership from:
Membership Department, P.O. Box 39, Bromley, Kent BR1 1NH.
or 36, Queen Anne's Gate, London SW1H 9AS.

Open To View tickets available to personal callers only from all LTB Tourist Information Centres.

HMS BELFAST

Symon's Wharf,
Off Tooley Street, SE1
Tel: 01-407 6434

London Bridge

London Bridge/Tower Hill, then ferry from Tower Pier (operates daily in summer, weekends in winter).

Explore all 7 decks of this Royal Navy cruiser and discover how sailors lived and worked at sea. Experience the Boiler and Engine Rooms, Messdecks, Cells, 6-inch guns and much more. Free talks, films, quiz sheets and birthday party facilities available to groups who book in advance with the Education Officer.

Open: daily 11.00–17.50 (16.30 in winter). **Admission charge.** CD under 16.

P d limited access

Vending area, picnics permitted on outer decks. Covered picnic area for up to 30 children (book in advance).

Combine with: London Dungeon, Tower Bridge, Tower of London, Kathleen and May Schooner, Hay's Galleria.

HMS Belfast

BETHNAL GREEN MUSEUM OF CHILDHOOD

Cambridge Heath Road, E2
Tel: 01-980 2415

Bethnal Green

The Victoria and Albert Museum's famous collection of doll's houses, dolls, toys, puppets, children's costumes, wedding dresses. Saturday school for painting and activities.

Open: Mon–Thurs and Sat 10.00–18.00, Sun 14.30–18.00. **Free.**

P on site WC Lift available, wheelchair entrance at back, help available. please phone in advance.

Combine with: Geffrye Museum, Whitechapel Art Gallery.

BOOKBOAT

Cutty Sark Gardens
Greenwich, SE10
Tel: 01-853 4383

Maze Hill/Greenwich

DLR Island Gardens

Boat from Westminster, Charing Cross or Tower Piers.

London's only floating children's bookshop.

Open: Mon–Wed, Fri–Sun 10.00–17.00.

P aa Restaurants and snack bars nearby.

Combine with: Cutty Sark, Gipsy Moth IV, National Maritime Museum, Old Royal Observatory, Thames Barrier. Weekend covered arts and crafts market Sat and Sun 10.30–16.30 all year.

BOOK TRUST

Book House
45 East Hill, SW18
Tel: 01-870 9055

Wandsworth Town

Here can be found the entire range of children's books for the last two years. Lovers of Beatrix Potter's books can also see some of her watercolours of nature studies, part of the Leslie Lindar Collection, by appointment only.

Open: Mon–Fri 09.00–17.00 (can close for lunch 13.00–14.00). **Free.**

BRASS RUBBING

A fascinating and interesting pastime. The following Brass Rubbing Centres have large collections of Mediaeval and Tudor brasses of knights, ladies, priests, children etc. A charge is made for rubbings and materials. **Admission Free.**

All Hallows By The Tower
Byward Street, EC3
Tel: 01-481 2928

⊖ Tower Hill

Open: Mon–Sat 11.00–17.45, Sun 12.30–17.45 (shorter hours in winter). Instruction given.

🅿 b

The Brass Rubbing Centre
Westminster Abbey, SW1
Tel: 01-222 2085

⊖ Westminster/St. James's Park

Open: Mon–Sat 09.00–17.00 (late opening Wednesday until 20.00 July and August).

🅿 p

Brass Rubbing Centre
St. Martin in the Fields Church,
Trafalgar Square
Tel: 01-437 6023

Open: Mon–Sat 10.00–18.00, Sun 12.00–18.00. Gift shop.

BRITISH MUSEUM

Great Russell Street, WC1
Tel: 01-636 1555

⊖ Tottenham Court Road/Goodge Street/Russell Square/Holborn

Egyptian mummies, The Elgin Marbles from the Parthenon, the Rosetta stone, the Sutton Hoo ship burial. Daily life in ancient Egypt, Greece and Rome. Life in Roman Britain. Oriental animal sculptures. Clocks through the ages.

Open: Mon–Sat 10.00–17.00, Sun 14.30–18.00.

🅿 g ♿ Lift available, avoiding front steps. Wheelchairs available. Please notify in advance.

✗ Cafeteria. Sandwiches may be eaten on colonnade outside museum.

Combine with: Pollock's Toy Museum, London Transport Museum.

BRUCE CASTLE MUSEUM

Lordship Lane, Tottenham, N17
Tel: 01-808 8772

⇌ ⊖ Seven Sisters

British Postal History. Local history.

Open: Daily incl. Sun 13.00–17.00.

Also houses the Museum of the Middlesex Regimental Association.

Open: Tues–Sat 13.00–17.00 (closed Sun and Mon). Bruce Castle closed winter Bank Holidays and Good Friday.

CABARET MECHANICAL THEATRE

33-34 The Market,
Covent Garden, WC2
Tel: 01-379 7961

⊖ Covent Garden

Exhibition of contemporary automata, all of which move at the touch of a button. Shop.

Open: Daily 10.00–19.00 (summer), Mon 12.00–18.30, Tues–Sun 10.00–18.30 (winter).
Admission charge. CD 16 and under. 5 and under **Free.**

🅿 k l ✗ Large choice of restaurants and cafes within the Covent Garden complex and nearby.

Combine with: Light Fantastic Gallery of Holography, London Transport Museum, Theatre Museum, British Museum.

CABINET WAR ROOMS

Clive Steps,
King Charles Street, SW1
Tel: 01-930 6961
01-735 8922 (Imperial War Museum)

⊖ Westminster

The Cabinet War Rooms are the surviving underground emergency accommodation provided for Churchill's War Cabinet and its chief military advisers during the Second World War. The Imperial War Museum has restored the War Rooms and turned them into a museum.

Open: Daily 10.00–17.50 (last admission 17.15).
Admission charge. CD under 16.

🅿 p ♿ ✗ Many restaurants in Victoria area.

Combine with: Changing the Guard, Queens Gallery, Royal Mews, St. James's Park.

CHANGING THE GUARD

The famous ceremony takes place at:

Buckingham Palace, SW1

⇌ Victoria

⊖ Victoria/St. James's Park.

11.30 alternate days (winter mid Aug–Mar). 11.30 daily (summer Apr–early Aug).

For dates telephone London Tourist Board 01-730 3488 (Mon–Fri 09.00–18.00).

Combine with: Queen's Gallery, Royal Mews.

Horse Guards Parade, Whitehall, SW1

⇌ Charing Cross

⊖ Westminster/Charing Cross

11.00 Mon–Sat, 10.00 Sun.

Combine with: Houses of Parliament, National Gallery, Westminster Abbey.

CHISLEHURST CAVES

Old Hill, Chislehurst, Kent Tel: 01-467 3264

⇌ Chislehurst

Miles of mysterious caverns with many interesting and exciting attractions for children including giant fossils, Haunted Pool.

Open: Summer daily 11.00–17.00, winter Sat and Sun 11.00–17.00. Tours. **Admission charge.** CD under 15.

P on site 🚐 nearby ⚹ bumpy terrain.

✕ Snack bar (open all year), cafe building with tables and chairs plus some picnic tables under cover.

COMMONWEALTH INSTITUTE

Kensington High Street, W8 Tel: 01-603 4535 🅻

⊖ High Street Kensington

Exhibitions on life in Commonwealth countries. Quiz sheets. Shop and library. School and holiday activities.

Open: Mon–Sat 10.00–17.30, Sun 14.00–17.00. **Free.**

P 🚐 on site ⚹

✕ Restaurant and coffee shop.

Combine with: Kensington Gardens, Kensington Palace.

CUTTY SARK

King William Walk, Greenwich Pier, SE10 Tel: 01-858 3445

⇌ Maze Hill/Greenwich

DLR Island Gardens

Boat from Westminster, Charing Cross and Tower Piers.

One of the most famous clipper ships. Collection of ships' figureheads. Sailor's cabin and galley with old furnishings. Explanatory labels to show how the rigging worked.

Open: Oct–March, Mon–Sat 10.00–17.00, Sun 12.00–17.00. April–Sept, Mon–Sat 10.00–18.00, Sun 12.00–18.00. **Admission charge.** CD Under 16.

P aa 🚐 bb ✕ Restaurants and snack bars nearby in Greenwich.

Combine with: Bookboat, Gipsy Moth IV, National Maritime Museum, Old Royal Observatory, Thames Barrier.

DICKENS' HOUSE

**48 Doughty Street, WC1
Tel: 01-405 2127**

🚇 Russell Square

Dickens' house from 1837–1839, during which time he worked on *Nicholas Nickleby, The Pickwick Papers* and *Oliver Twist*. The house contains letters, pictures, first editions, manuscripts and room settings of the period.

Open: Mon–Sat 10.00–17.00 (last admission 16.30) closed Bank Holidays.
Admission charge. 🆑 16.

Combine with: British Museum.

DULWICH PICTURE GALLERY

**College Road, SE21
Tel: 01-693 5254**

🚆 West Dulwich/North Dulwich

First purpose-built art gallery (Soane) with outstanding collection of paintings by the Old Masters: Rembrandt, Van de Welde, Gainsborough. Picture trail, quizzes and colouring sheets.

Open: Tue–Sat 10.00–13.00, 14.00–17.00; Sun 14.00–17.00.
Admission charge.

🚗 on site 🚻 ✕ Dulwich Park and Village.

Combine with: Crystal Palace Park, Horniman Museum.

GEFFRYE MUSEUM

**Kingsland Road, E2
Tel: 01-739 8368**

🚆 🚇 Liverpool Street then bus
🚆 🚇 Old Street then bus

English furniture and decorative arts in a series of room settings (1600–1939), 18th century woodworker's shop, open hearth kitchen, small but interesting collection of paintings.

Open: Tues–Sat and Bank Holiday Mons 10.00–17.00, Sun 14.00–17.00. **Free.**

📍 in the surrounding streets 🚻

✕ Coffee bar.

Combine with: Bethnal Green Museum of Childhood, Tower Bridge, Tower of London.

GIPSY MOTH IV

**King William Walk,
Greenwich Pier, SE10
Tel: 01-858 3445**

🚆 Maze Hill/Greenwich

DLR Island Gardens

Boat from Westminster, Charing Cross and Tower Piers.

The boat in which Sir Francis Chichester sailed single-handed around the world in 1966.

Open: Mon–Sat 10.30–18.00, Sun and Good Friday 12.00–18.00 (April–Oct).
Admission charge. 🆑 Under 16.

📍 aa 🚗 bb ✕ Restaurants and snack bars nearby in Greenwich.

Combine with: Bookboat, Cutty Sark, National Maritime Museum, Old Royal Observatory, Thames Barrier.

GUINNESS WORLD OF RECORDS

**The Trocadero Centre,
Piccadilly Circus, W1
Tel: 01-439 7331/5 or 01-367 4567**

🚇 Piccadilly Circus/Leicester Square

This exciting Exhibition, using videos, computers and life-sized models, brings to life many of the amazing and varied facts from the Guinness Book of Records. The Exhibition has six themed areas which correspond to the main sections of the book: The Human World; The Animal World; Our Planet Earth; Structures & Machines; Sports World; The World of Entertainment and Great British Achievements. Gift Shop.

Open: Daily 10.00–21.30.
Admission charge. Under 4's Free.
🆑 Under 15.

📍 i m 🚻 Staff operated lift facilities.

✕ Many restaurants within the Trocadero Centre.

Combine with: Light Fantastic, London Experience within Trocadero complex.

HAMPTON COURT PALACE

East Molesey, Surrey
Tel: 01-977 8441

⇌ Hampton Court

Green Line bus 715, 718. Boat from Westminster Pier and Kingston (summer only)

Built in 1514 for Cardinal Wolsey, then became one of Henry VIII's royal palaces. State apartments, picture gallery, Tudor tennis court and kitchens, Great Vine and Maze.

Open: Palace (April–Sept) Mon–Sat 09.30–18.00, Sun 11.00–18.00. (Oct–March) Mon–Sat 09.30–17.00, Sun 14.00–17.00. Maze (March–Oct daily 10.00–17.00. Kitchens and tennis court (April–Sept only) times as for Palace.
Admission charge (last admission ½ hour before closing). CD Under 16. Under 5s **Free.**

P on site 🚐 Western end at Hampton Court Green.

♿ Access to first floor State apartments by prior arrangement.

✗ Tilt Yard Restaurant, cafeteria, picnicking in the grounds and by the river.

Combine with: Bushey Park.

HEATHROW AIRPORT TERMINAL TWO ROOF GARDENS

Hounslow, Middlesex
Tel: 01-759 4321

⊖ Heathrow Terminal 1, 2, 3

Open-air area from which you can watch the planes take off and land at this busy international airport. Telescopes available.

Open: Daily 09.30–16.30.
Admission charge. CD Under 15.
P 🚐 on site ♿ ✗ Cafeteria.

HORNIMAN MUSEUM

100 London Road, SE23
Tel: 01-699 2339

⇌ Forest Hill

Ethnographic collections illustrate man's beliefs, arts and crafts, musical instruments, weapons and tools. Natural History collections display mammals, birds, reptiles, fish, invertebrates, a beehive and an aquarium. Education Centre. Totem Pole in garden.

Open: Mon–Sat 10.30–18.00, Sun 14.00–18.00. Horniman Workshop Open: Sat and ILEA school holidays 10.30–12.30, 13.30–15.30. Minimum age 8. **Free.** (Closed 24, 25, 26 Dec.)

P 🚐 Street parking in Sydenham Rise.

♿ ✗ Tea Rooms (afternoons). Picnic area in adjoining Horniman Gardens. Cafes in Forest Hill 10 mins, walk away.

Combine with: Crystal Palace Park, Dulwich Picture Gallery.

19

HOUSES OF PARLIAMENT

St. Margaret Street, SW1
Tel: 01-219 3090

⊖ Westminster

House of Lords, House of Commons, Strangers' Galleries, The famous bell, Big Ben, is in the Clock Tower (not open to the public).

Please note: The Palace of Westminster and Westminster Hall are not open to the general public except for debates. Visits to the Palace of Westminster may only be made by arrangement with a member of Parliament or Peer.

Debates: Admission to the Strangers' Galleries is either by advance application to your MP, a Peer, or through your embassy or by joining a queue at St. Stephen's entrance. Admission is from 16.15 Mon–Thurs and 10.00 Fri. (Commons) and from 14.40 Tues, Wed, Thurs, and some Mon (Lords). **Free.**

P p

&. Route through Commons and Lords is on first floor level. Please notify Member who is arranging permit in advance so that arrangements can be made to transport wheelchairs to this level.

✗ Small snack bars and restaurants nearby.

Combine with: Cabinet War Rooms, Changing the Guard (Horse Guards Parade), National Gallery, National Portrait Gallery, Westminster Abbey.

IMPERIAL WAR MUSEUM

Lambeth Road, SE1
Tel: 01-735 8922 **L**

⊖ Lambeth North

British aircraft from World Wars I and II. One-man submarine, models of warships, uniforms, guns and tanks. V-2 rocket. Photographs, paintings, explanatory displays and models. Public film shows at weekends and during school holidays. The museum is at present undergoing re-development.

Open: Mon–Sat 10.00–17.50, Sun 14.00–17.50. **Free.**

P Meter parking &. use of lift

✗ Vending machines in museum. Packed lunches may be eaten in vending machine area. Picnicking in next door park.

Combine with: HMS Belfast, London Dungeon, Kathleen and May Schooner.

THE INTERNATIONAL STOCK EXCHANGE

Old Broad Street, EC2
Tel: 01-588 2355 **L**

⊖ Bank

Stock Exchange Information Officers explain the work of the Exchange. A colour film about the Stock Exchange is shown at regular intervals throughout the day. Parties of up to 20 can reserve seats by writing or phoning in advance.

Open: Mon–Fri 09.45–17.00. **Free.**

P a

&. Business entrance and lift may be used. Please notify in advance.

✗ Numerous restaurants and snack bars nearby in the City; many are closed Sat and Sun.

Combine with: Lloyd's, Mansion House, Monument, Museum of London, National Postal Museum, St. Paul's Cathedral.

KATHLEEN & MAY SCHOONER

St. Mary Overy Dock, off Cathedral Street, SE1 Tel: 01-403 3965 or 01-730 0096

≠ ⊖ London Bridge

Traditional wooden three-masted topsail schooner, built in 1900, which used to carry cargoes of all kinds around the coasts of Britain and sometimes across the Channel. Exhibition on board with video film and sound effects.

Open daily: 10.00–15.00, 16.00 or 17.00. **Admission charge.** Under 5s **Free.** CD Under 16.

P d

Combine with: HMS Belfast, Tower Bridge, London Dungeon.

KENSINGTON PALACE

The Broad Walk, Kensington Gardens, W8 Tel: 01-937 9561

⊖ High Street Kensington/Queensway

State apartments of the late Stuart and Hanoverian periods; mainly 17th century furniture and pictures. See Queen Victoria's bedroom, her mothers' dressing room, some of Queen Victoria's toys. Court Dress collection on loan from HM The Queen, shows suits and uniforms worn at the British Court from the late 19th century onwards. The Princess of Wales' wedding dress is here (for 2 years 1987/1988).

Open: Mon–Sat 09.00–17.00, Sun 13.00–17.00. **Admission charge.** Under 5s free. CD Under 16.

P v ✗ Restaurants and cafes nearby in Kensington and Queensway. Picnicking in Kensington Gardens.

Combine with: Commonwealth Institute, Kensington Gardens, London Toy and Model Museum, Queens Ice Skating Rink.

KEW BRIDGE STEAM MUSEUM

Green Dragon Lane, Kew Bridge Road, Brentford, Middlesex Tel: 01-568 4757

≠ Kew Bridge

⊖ Gunnersbury then bus 237, 267

Boat from Westminster Pier to Kew Gardens (summer only)

A pumping station with six huge steam-driven water pumping engines in working order and other steam-driven pumping engines on display. Steam railway, diesel house and water supply exhibits.

Open: In Steam, Sat and Sun and Bank Holiday Mondays 11.00–17.00. Static exhibition Mon–Fri 11.00–17.00. **Admission charge.** Under 5s free. CD under 16.

P 🚌 on site ♿ ✗ Tea Room

Combine with: Kew Gardens, Syon House and Gardens.

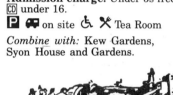

LIGHT FANTASTIC GALLERY OF HOLOGRAPHY

48 South Row, The Market, Covent Garden, WC2 Tel: 01-836 6423/4

⊖ Covent Garden

A changing display of some of the world's most advanced holograms.

Open: Mon–Wed 10.00–18.00, Thurs and Fri 10.00–20.00, Sat 10.00–19.00, Sun 11.00–18.00. **Admission charge.** CD Under 16.

P k l ✗ Restaurants and snack bars nearby

Combine with: Cabaret Mechanical Theatre, London Transport Museum, Theatre Museum, British Museum.

LIGHT FANTASTIC "COME TOUCH TOMORROW"

**The Trocadero, Coventry Street, W1
Tel: 01-734 4516**

Θ Piccadilly Circus

The largest hologram in the world on display at the largest exhibition of holography in the world.

Open daily 10.00–22.00. **Admission charge.** CD under 16.

P i m X Restaurants within Trocadero complex.

Combine with: Guinness World of Records, London Experience (also within Trocadero complex).

LLOYD'S OF LONDON

**Lime Street, EC3
Tel: 01-623 7100
(Visitors' Information)**

⇌ Fenchurch Street

Θ Bank/Monument

Lloyd's is an international insurance market. Ride in a glass lift up to a multimedia exhibition which traces the history of Lloyd's. The Viewing Gallery overlooks the famous Underwriting Room and the Lutine Bell.

Open: Mon–Fri 10.00–14.30 (10.00–15.45 for pre-booked parties).

P b & X Coffee House

Combine with: Monument, Museum of London, International Stock Exchange, Tower of London.

LONDON DUNGEON

**28/34 Tooley Street, SE1
Tel: 01-403 0606**

⇌ Θ London Bridge

The world's first mediaeval horror museum in huge, dark vaults under London Bridge station.

Open: Daily 10.00–17.30 (April–Sept). 10.00–16.30 (Oct–March).
Admission charge. CD Under 14.
Not recommended for sensitive children.

P d & X Cafeteria. Small area of tables and chairs immediately adjoining the Coffee Shop, also a number of long bench seats throughout the exhibition for small party gatherings.

Combine with: HMS Belfast, Imperial War Museum, Tower Bridge, Kathleen and May Schooner.

THE LONDON EXPERIENCE

**Trocadero Centre
Piccadilly Circus, W1
Tel: 01-439 4938/01-734 0555**

Θ Piccadilly Circus/Leicester Square

A spectacular multi-screen, audio-visual entertainment portraying the sights and sounds of London old and new. Continuous performances every 40 minutes between 10.20 and 22.20.

P i m & X in Trocadero complex.

Combine with: Guinness World of Records, Light Fantastic, within Trocadero complex.

LONDON TOY AND MODEL MUSEUM

**October House,
23 Craven Hill, W2
Tel: 01-262 9450**

Θ Bayswater/Paddington/Queensway

Museum containing one of the world's finest collections of toys and working models. Large garden with operating model railways, a ride-on railway for children, antique roundabout and vintage bus.

Open: Tues–Sat 10.00–17.30, Sun 11.00–17.30.
Admission charge. CD Under 16.

P w x X Refreshments, cafeteria.

Combine with: Kensington Gardens, Kensington Palace.

LONDON TRANSPORT MUSEUM

Covent Garden, WC2
Tel: 01-379 6344

⊖ Covent Garden/Leicester Square

Horse-drawn omnibuses, trolleybuses, trams, railway locomotives and rolling stock illustrate the development of London's public passenger transport system since 1829. Visitors can "drive" a modern bus, a tram and a tube train and work points and signals in a section of tunnel. A new simulator shows a driver's eye-view of a trip round the Circle line. Video displays and many fine models. New museum shop. Children's activity sheets.

Open: Daily 10.00–18.00.
Admission charge. Under 5's **Free.** CD 16.

P k l ♿ ✗ Refreshments (three station benches are available for visitors to eat packed lunches – normally allocated to groups for specific periods on busy days by the attendants).

Combine with: Cabaret Mechanical Theatre, Light Fantastic Gallery of Holography, Theatre Museum, British Museum.

MADAME TUSSAUD'S

Marylebone Road, NW1
Tel: 01-935 6861

⊖ Baker Street

Wax figures of famous people, historical characters, film stars, pop singers, sportsmen, politicians, etc. Chamber of Horrors with murderers, hangmen and assassins. Tableaux of The Little Princes in the Tower, The Battle of Trafalgar and a Sleeping Beauty who breathes even though she's made of wax! Gift shop.

Open: Mon–Fri 10.00–17.30, Sat and Sun and Bank Holidays 09.30–17.30.
Admission charge. CD Under 16.

P e ♿ Not at busy periods. Please notify in advance.

✗ Snack bars.

Combine with: Planetarium, London Zoo.

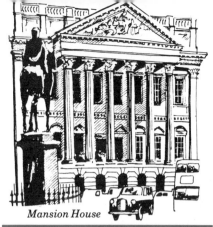

Mansion House

MANSION HOUSE

Mansion House Street, EC4
Tel: 01-626 2500

⊖ Bank

The London official residence of the Lord Mayor of London. Arrangements can be made for group visits only (minimum age 12) on Tues, Wed and Thurs at 11.00 or 14.00 by written appointment only. **Free.**

P a ✗ Numerous restaurants and snack bars in the City but many are closed on Sat and Sun.

Combine with: Lloyd's, Monument, Museum of London, National Postal Museum, Old Bailey, St. Paul's Cathedral, International Stock Exchange.

MONUMENT

Monument Street, EC3
Tel: 01-626 2717

⊖ Monument/Bank

A 17th century hollow column designed by Wren, 202 feet high because it stands 202 feet from the site of the baker's shop in Pudding Lane where the Great Fire of London began in 1666. There are 311 steps – but no lift! – and a wonderful view can be enjoyed from the top.

Open: (April–Sept) Mon–Fri 09.00–17.40, Sat and Sun 14.00–17.40, (Oct–March) Mon–Sat 09.00–15.40. Advisable to ring before visiting.
Admission charge. CD Under 16.

P b ✗ Numerous restaurants and snack bars nearby in the City although many are closed on Sat and Sun.

Combine with: Lloyd's, Mansion House, Museum of London, National Postal Museum, Old Bailey, St. Paul's Cathedral, International Stock Exchange, Tower Bridge, Tower of London.

MOUNTFITCHET CASTLE

Bayley Walls, Stansted Mountfitchet, Essex
Tel: (0279) 813237/815035

≢ Stansted (100 yards away)

Reconstruction of Mountfitchet Castle (a Norman wooden motte and bailey castle and village of 1066) on its original site.

Open: daily 10.00–17.30.
Admission charge.

P 🚐 Free

✗ Picnic area and covered seating for 40.

MUSEUM OF ARTILLERY IN THE ROTUNDA

Woolwich Common, SE18
Tel: 01-854 2242 Ext. 3127

≢ ⊖ New Cross/New Cross Gate then bus 53, 54, 75

⊖ Woolwich Arsenal, then bus

A marvellous collection of old guns.

Open: Mon–Fri 12.00–17.00, (16.00 winter) Sat and Sun 13.00–17.00 (16.00 winter).
Free.

P Adjacent Museum 🚐 75 yards from Museum.

♿ Limited facilities ✗ Cold drinks available, picnicking in grounds.

Combine with: Cutty Sark, Gipsy Moth IV, National Maritime Museum, Old Royal Observatory, Thames Barrier.

MUSEUM OF LONDON

London Wall, EC2
Tel: 01-600 3699

≢ Moorgate

⊖ St. Paul's/Barbican (closed Sun)/Moorgate

The history of London from pre-historic times to the present day. Roman London, Mediaeval London, Tudor and Stuart London, models and room reconstructions from every period, 18th century prison cells, model of the Great Fire of London with lighting and sound effects, the Lord Mayor's Coach, Georgian, Victorian and 20th century galleries, temporary exhibitions. Children's quizzes, school holiday activities.

Open: Tues–Sat 10.00–18.00, Sun 14.00–18.00. **Free.**

P a 🚐 on site for pre-booked parties only.

♿ Public slopes and walkways onto the Highwalk from Moorgate. Public lift from street level to Highwalk level in Aldersgate Street. Wheelchairs (and pushchairs) available.

✗ Coffee shop with snacks. Benches outside, under cover for picnicking.

Combine with: Lloyd's, Mansion House, Monument, National Postal Museum, Old Bailey, St. Paul's Cathedral, International Stock Exchange.

MUSEUM OF MANKIND

Burlington Gardens, W1
Tel: 01-437 2224

⊖ Piccadilly Circus/Green Park

The Ethnography department of the British Museum. The museum has displays showing the life and culture of peoples of many lands. Current exhibitions include Madagascar: Island of the Ancestors, Bolivian Worlds, and Treasurers from the Ethnographic Collection. Exhibitions are changed from time to time so check for the latest details. Work sheets are available and there are film shows Tues–Fri. Groups should contact the Information Desk in advance.

Open: Mon–Sat 10.00–17.00, Sun 14.30–18.00. **Free.**

P h ♿ Lift available ✗ Restaurants and cafes near Piccadilly Circus.

Combine with: Guinness World of Records, Light Fantastic Gallery of Holography, and London Experience (all within Trocadero complex, Piccadilly Circus).

NATIONAL ARMY MUSEUM

Royal Hospital Road, SW3
Tel: 01-730 0717

⊖ Sloane Square then short walk
Bus 39 (Mon–Sat only)

The history of the British Army from 1485. Arms and armour, uniforms, the skeleton of Napoleon's horse "Marengo", a lamp traditionally used by Florence Nightingale. Summer holiday activities for young people aged 7 upwards, include model making, drawing, trails, films and talks. Further information is available each July from the Education Department. Please enclose a SAE.

Open: Mon–Sat 10.00–17.30, Sun 14.00–17.30. **Free.**

P r 🚐 Coach lay-by ♿

✗ Museum cafeteria (packed lunches may be eaten here).

Combine with: Battersea Park.

NATIONAL GALLERY

Trafalgar Square, WC2
Tel: 01-839 3321/3526

⇌ ⊖ Charing Cross

A huge collection with examples from West European Schools of painting from ca. 1300 to ca. 1900. Special guided tours and quiz sheets are available during the Christmas, Easter and Summer holidays. Talks and worksheets for school groups by arrangement with the Education Department.

Open: Mon–Sat 10.00–18.00, Sun 14.00–18.00. **Free.**

P k ♿ Rear entrance in Orange Street, lift available. Please phone in advance.

✗ Restaurant.

Combine with: Changing the Guard (Horse Guards Parade), National Portrait Gallery.

NATIONAL MARITIME MUSEUM

Romney Road, Greenwich, SE10
Tel: 01-858 4422 ext. 221

⇌ Maze Hill

⊖ and DLR Island Gardens

Boat from Westminster, Charing Cross, Tower and Festival Piers.

The history of Britain and the sea at peace and at war. See Nelson's Trafalgar uniform, royal state barges, ship models and naval weapons. Climb aboard a paddle steamer and trace the development of the ship through the ages.

Open: Mon–Sat 10.00–18.00 (17.00 in winter), Sun 14.00–18.00 (17.00 in winter). **Admission charge.** Under 7s free.
[CD] Under 16.

P z 🚐 bb ♿ Please phone in advance.

✗ Restaurant, picnicking in the grounds.

Combine with: Cutty Sark, Gipsy Moth IV, Old Royal Observatory, Thames Barrier.

NATIONAL PORTRAIT GALLERY

St. Martin's Place, WC2
Tel: 01-930 1552

⇌ Charing Cross

⊖ Charing Cross/Leicester Square

Portraits of the famous and infamous from the Tudors to today; sovereigns, sportsmen, scientists, stars of the stage and screen. Temporary exhibitions. Quiz and worksheets. Special holiday events.

Open: Mon–Sat 10.00–17.00, Sat 10.00–18.00, Sun 14.00–18.00.

P k ♿ Entrance in Orange Street, lift available. Please phone in advance.

✗ Restaurants and snack bars nearby.

Combine with: Changing the Guard (Horse Guards Parade), National Gallery.

NATIONAL POSTAL MUSEUM

King Edward Street, EC1
Tel: 01-432 3851

⊖ St. Paul's

The history of the postage stamp in Britain. A complete collection of British stamps and a large selection from other countries.

Open: Mon–Thurs 10.00–16.30, Fri 10.00–16.00. **Free.**

P c ♿ Difficult. Party arrangements only can be made. Please telephone in advance.

✗ Restaurants and snack bars nearby in the City.

Combine with: Lloyd's, Mansion House, Museum of London, Old Bailey, St. Paul's Cathedral, International Stock Exchange.

NATURAL HISTORY MUSEUM

Cromwell Road, SW7
Tel: 01-589 6323
⊖ South Kensington

The museum contains the national collections of living and fossil plants and animals, rocks, minerals and meteorites. Exhibitions include Human Biology, Introducing Ecology, Dinosaurs and their living relatives, man's place in Evolution, Origin of Species, British Natural History and Introducing Mammals. The Information Desk is open most days throughout the year. It offers advice on how best to spend your time in the Museum, and a wide range of activity sheets are available for use during your visit. The Family Centre is open during the Easter and summer holidays.

Open: Mon–Sat 10.00–18.00, Sun 13.00–18.00.
Admission charge (free admission 16.30–18.00, Mon–Fri. except Bank Holidays).

P u ♿ Please notify in advance ✗ Snack bars and cafeteria.

Combine with: Kensington Gardens, Science Museum, Victoria and Albert Museum.

NELSON'S COLUMN

Trafalgar Square, WC2
⇌ Charing Cross
⊖ Charing Cross/Embankment

Granite column 167 feet, 5½ inches high with a statute of Nelson 17 feet 4½ inches high. The four lions at the base of the column are made of bronze and were designed by Sir Edward Landseer.

P k m ♿ From south side of square.

✗ Restaurants and snack bars nearby.

Combine with: Changing the Guard (Horse Guards Parade), National Gallery, National Portrait Gallery.

NORTH WOOLWICH OLD STATION MUSEUM

Pier Road, North Woolwich, E16
Tel: 01-474 7244
⇌ North Woolwich

Museum showing the history of the Great Eastern Railway. Reconstructed booking office and platform canopy of 1910, rolling stock, three locomotives, photographs and three model locomotives.

Open: Mon–Sat 10.00–17.00, Sun and bank holidays 14.00–17.00. **Free.**

OLD BAILEY

Old Bailey, EC4
Tel: 01-248 3277
⇌ Holborn Viaduct
⊖ St. Paul's

The site of Old Newgate Prison, now the Central Criminal Court. There is a statue of Justice on top of the dome. When the courts are in session, the public galleries are open from 10.15–13.00 and 14.00–16.30 Mon to Fri. You are requested not to take packages or large bags with you when visiting the Old Bailey. Tape recorders and cameras are not permitted. (Minimum age for visitors 14). **Free.**

P c ✗ Snack bars nearby.

Combine with: Lloyd's, Mansion House, Monument, Museum of London, National Postal Museum, St. Paul's Cathedral, International Stock Exchange.

OLD ROYAL OBSERVATORY

**Greenwich Park, SE10
Tel: 01-858 4422 Ext. 221**

≋ Maze Hill

⊖ and DLR Island Gardens

Boat from Westminster, Charing Cross, Tower Pier and Festival Piers.

The original home of Greenwich Mean Time and past Astronomers Royal. Stand astride the Greenwich Meridien and see the "Time Ball" drop at 13.00 every day. Fascinating collection of historic timekeepers, telescopes and navigational instruments, Planetarium plus the largest refracting telescope in Britain.

Open: Mon–Sat 10.00–18.00 (17.00 in winter), Sun 14.00–18.00 (17.00 in winter). **Admission charge.** Under 7s free. CD Under 16.

P cc 🚌 cc ✕ Park Restaurant, picnicking on Blackheath and in Greenwich Park.

Combine with: Bookboat, Cutty Sark, Gipsy Moth IV, National Maritime Museum, Thames Barrier.

PLANETARIUM/ LASERIUM

**Marylebone Road, NW1
Tel: 01-486 1121**

⊖ Baker Street

The Zeiss Star Projector transports you through space and time. There are presentations throughout the day. Astronomers exhibition, Laserium Light concerts accompanied by rock and pop music in the evenings. For details phone 01-486 2242.

Open: Daily 11.00–16.30. **Admission charge.** CD Under 16.

P e ✕ Snack bar.

Combine with: London Zoo, Madame Tussauds.

POLLOCK'S TOY MUSEUM

**1 Scala Street, W1
Tel: 01-636 3452**

⊖ Goodge Street

Victorian toy theatres, peep shows, optical toys, old dolls, doll's houses and teddy bears, folk toys. Cut-out theatres, miniatures and old fashioned toys on sale.

Open: Mon–Sat 10.00–17.00. **Admission charge.** CD Under 18.

P g ✕ Snack bars nearby.

Combine with: British Museum.

QUEEN'S GALLERY

**Buckingham Palace Road, SW1
Tel: 01-930 3007 Ext. 430**

≋ ⊖ Victoria

Exhibition of paintings and other items from the Royal collections.

Open: Tues–Sat 10.30–17.00, Sun 14.00–17.00. **Admission charge.** CD Under 16.

P r ♿ Ground floor only.

✕ Restaurants and snack bars nearby, picnicking in St. James's Park.

Combine with: Changing the Guard (Buckingham Palace), Royal Mews, St. James's Park, Cabinet War Rooms.

ROYAL AIR FORCE MUSEUM

Grahame Park Way, Hendon, NW9
Tel: 01-205 2266

⊖ Colindale then 15 minutes walk.

Museum of the Royal Air Force with real aircraft, including scale models of all aircraft ever flown by the RAF. The building incorporates 2 hangars of 1915. The history of military flying, uniforms of famous and Royal fliers, radar, guns, airships, etc. **Free.**

Nearby is the:

BATTLE OF BRITAIN MUSEUM

Houses a unique collection of British, German and Italian aircraft which fought in the Battle of Britain. Spitfire, Hurricane, Heinkel, Gladiator, Defiant, Blenheim, Messerschmitt, Junkers and Fiat. Uniforms, medals, relics, documents, works of art and other memorabilia from the Battle of Britain.
Admission charge.

Adjacent is the:

BOMBER COMMAND MUSEUM

Which contains a striking display of bomber aircraft including the Vulcan, Valiant, Lancaster and Mosquito.
Admission charge.

All 3 museums open: Mon–Sat 10.00–18.00, Sun 14.00–18.00. CD Under 16.

P 🚐 on site ♿ Lifts available.

✗ Restaurant and picnic building (seats up to 50).

ROYAL MEWS

Buckingham Palace Road, SW1
Tel: 01-930 4832

⇌ ⊖ Victoria

The Queen's Horses, The Royal and State Coaches including Gold Coach, Glass Coach, Irish State Coach etc.

Open: Wed and Thurs 14.00–16.00 (except on state occasions and during Ascot week). **Admission charge.** CD Under 16.

P r ♿ ✗ Restaurants and cafes nearby, picnicking in St. James's Park.

Combine with: Changing the Guard (Buckingham Palace), Queen's Gallery, Cabinet War Rooms.

ROYALTY AND EMPIRE

Windsor and Eton Central Station, Thames Street, Windsor, Berkshire
Tel: (0753) 857837

The colourful exhibition recreates the magnificence of Queen Victoria's 1897 Diamond Jubilee celebrations in a new and exciting way. Experience the stirring sight and sounds of history being made in the splendid original surroundings, only yards from Windsor Castle. The astonishing, fully automated theatre show (no extra charge) actually brings famous Victorians to life, using techniques seen for the first time in Britain and Europe.

Open: Daily 09.30–17.30 (16.30 in winter).

✗ Outside buffet area serving light snacks (summer only).

Combine with: Windsor Castle, Windsor Safari Park.

RAF Museum

ST. PAUL'S CATHEDRAL

Ludgate Hill, EC4
Tel: 01-248 2705

⊖ St. Paul's

Built by Sir Christopher Wren in 1675–1710 to replace the old cathedral destroyed in the great Fire of London. The third largest Christian church in the world; in the magnificent dome is the Whispering Gallery. It is better not to visit the cathedral on Sundays unless you wish to attend a service. Holy Communion is at 08.00 and 11.30, Matins at 10.30 and Evensong at 15.15.

Open: Cathedral Mon–Sat 07.30–18.00, Sun 08.00–18.00 Crypt and Galleries Mon–Fri 10.00–16.15, Sat 11.00–16.15. Cathedral may be closed for special services. **Admission charge.** CD Under 16.

🅿 c ♿ ✗ Numerous restaurants and cafes nearby in the city, though many are closed on Sat and Sun.

Combine with: Lloyd's, Mansion House, Museum of London, National Postal Museum, International Stock Exchange.

SCIENCE MUSEUM

Exhibition Road, SW7
Tel: 01-589 3456

⊖ South Kensington

Exhibits outline the history of science and industry and include machines and models operated by push buttons, the Foucoult Pendulum which shows the rotation of the earth, famous locomotives, old carriages, cars and aircraft, the history of medicine. There are new galleries and The Exploration of Space and "Launch Pad" – a hands-on inter-active gallery for children.

Open: Mon–Sat 10.00–18.00, Sun 14.30–18.00. **Free.**

🅿 u ♿ Please telephone in advance.

✗ Cafeteria. Arrangements can be made for school parties to eat sandwiches in Museum. Please telephone in advance.

Combine with: Kensington Gardens, Natural History Museum, Victoria and Albert Museum.

SHAKESPEARE GLOBE MUSEUM

1 Bear Gardens, Bankside,
Southwark, SE1
Tel: 01-928 6342

🚇 London Bridge

⊖ London Bridge/Mansion House

Elizabethan theatre history, including a reconstruction of Shakespeare's first Globe theatre. Special events and activities for children. Phone for details of opening hours. **Admission charge.** CD Under 16.

🅿 on site ♿ Limited.

Replica Globe Theatre under construction nearby.

SOUTHALL RAILWAY CENTRE

Southall, Middlesex

🚇 Southall

Private goods station, static display of old steam and diesel locomotives and rolling stock. Small railway relic museum, operational on some weekends. Reopening 1988 – phone LTB for details.

SYON HOUSE AND PARK

Brentford, Middlesex
Tel: 01-560 0882

≈ Syon Lane

⊖ Gunnersbury then buses 237, 267 to Brent Lea Gate.

Gardens landscaped by Capability Brown. The Great Conservatory houses an aquarium and aviary.

Open: April–Sep daily 10.00–18.00; Oct–March 10.00–dusk.
Admission charge. Under 5's **Free.**
CD Under 17.

Syon House is the historic home of the Duke of Northumberland designed by Robert Adam.

Open: April 1st–end Sep, Sun–Thur 12.00–17.00; Oct Sun only 12.00–17.00 (last admission 16.15).
Admission charge. Under 5's **Free.**
CD Under 17.

The Heritage Motor Museum is the largest collection of British cars in the world. Over 100 cars on permanent display from 1895 to present day. Many prototypes plus production cars.

Open: April–Oct daily 10.00–17.30; Nov–March daily 10.00–16.00.
Admission charge. Under 5's **Free.**
CD Under 16.

The London Butterfly House contains live butterflies, giant spiders, leaf cutting ants, locusts and many other small insects.

Open: 10.00–17.00 (15.00 in winter).
Admission charge. Under 5's **Free.**
CD Under 16.

Art Centre and Garden Centre.

P 🚐 on site ✕ Restaurant, cafeteria. Picnicking in the grounds.

Combine with: Kew Bridge Steam Museum, Richmond Park.

TATE GALLERY

Millbank, SW1 Tel: 01-821 7128
(Recorded information)
01-821 1313

⊖ Pimlico

The Tate Gallery comprises the national collections of British painting and 20th century painting and sculpture, also Clore Gallery, housing the Turner Collection. Free lectures and films, special children's activities during most school holidays. Free guided tours of the gallery Mon to Fri. All school group visits **must** be booked in advance with the Education Department.

Open: Mon–Sat 10.00–17.50, Sun 14.00–17.50. **Free.**

P 4 hour meters, o, y 🚐 y

& WC at Atterbury Street entrance (wheelchairs on loan).

✕ Coffee shop and restaurant.

Combine with: Queen's Gallery, Royal Mews, Westminster Abbey.

TELECOM TECHNOLOGY SHOWCASE

135 Queen Victoria Street, EC4
Tel: 01-248 7444

≈ ⊖ Blackfriars

A complete history of telecommunications in Britain and a look forward to the future. Period covered: 19th and 20th century. Souvenir and bookshop.

Open Mon–Fri 10.00–17.00. Closed Bank Holidays. **Free.**

P NCP under building &

✕ Numerous snack bars nearby

THAMES BARRIER VISITORS CENTRE

Unity Way (off Woolwich Rd) SE18
Tel: 01-854 1373

≈ Charlton

ACCESS BY RIVER from three piers using 3 separate boat companies:

From Westminster, London Launches (01-740 8263); Westminster and Tower, Beta Boats (01-305 0888); Greenwich, Campion Launches (01-305 0300).

BUSES from Greenwich 51, 96, 161, 177, 180.

Adjacent to the Thames Barrier, the centre offers the best overall view of London's flood defence system. Attractions include an audio-visual presentation and exhibition highlighting the need for and explaining the workings of the Barrier. Souvenir shop.

Open Mon–Fri 10.30–17.00, (17.30 Sat & Sun). Closed 25, 26 Dec and 1 Jan.
Admission charge.

P 🚐 on site &

✕ Cafeteria on site. (Ground floor room available for eating packed lunches – additional space 500 yards off site).

Combine with: Cutty Sark, Gipsy Moth IV, National Maritime Museum, Old Royal Observatory.

THEATRE MUSEUM

**1E Tavistock Street,
(public entrance in Russell Street),
Covent Garden, WC2
Tel: 01-836 7891**

⊖ Covent Garden/Leicester Square

Five galleries illustrate the history of theatre, ballet and dance, rock and pop, circus, puppetry, the opera and musical stage. The exhibits are from the V&A museum's own collection and include costume, jewellery, props, engravings and playbills. Lectures, workshops and performances take place in the 85 seat auditorium. Shop: "First Call" theatre booking facilities.

Open: Galleries Tues–Sun 11.00–19.00; Shop, cafe bar, ticket agency Tues–Sat 11.00–20.00, Sun 11.00–19.00.
Admission charge. CD Under 15, under 5's **Free.**

P k l ♿ ✗ Cafe bar.

Combine with: Cabaret Mechanical Theatre, Light Fantastic Gallery of Holography, London Transport Museum, British Museum.

TOWER BRIDGE

**Tower Bridge, SE1
Tel: 01-407 0922**

⊖ Tower Hill

DLR Tower Gateway

Massive Victorian steam pumping engines, superb views over London from the glassed-in walkways, exhibitions, museum and shop.

Open: daily 10.00–18.30 (April–Oct), 10.00–16.45 (Nov–March). Last admission 45 minutes before closing.
Admission charge. CD Under 15.

P b 🚐 b ♿ Lift up to walkway.

Combine with: HMS Belfast, Tower of London, London Dungeon, Kathleen & May Schooner.

HM TOWER OF LONDON

**Tower Hill, EC3
Tel: 01-709 0765**

⊖ Tower Hill

DLR Tower Gateway

The Crown Jewels. The largest collection of early weapons and armour in Britain, including Henry VIII's armour, horse armour and armour for elephants. The block and axe with which executions were carried out. Traitors Gate, the Tower ravens, the Royal Fusiliers Museum, and souvenir shop.

Open: March–Oct Mon–Sat 09.30–17.45, last admission 17.00, Sun 14.00–17.45, last admission 17.00. Nov–Feb Mon–Sat 09.30–16.30, last admission 16.00, Sun Closed. NB The Jewel House is closed in February for the annual cleaning of the Crown Jewels.
Admission charge. CD Under 16.

P b 🚐 b ♿ To grounds only.

✗ Cafeteria and snack bar. Covered seating area for picnicking and picnicking by the river.

Combine with: HMS Belfast, Tower Bridge.

VICTORIA AND ALBERT MUSEUM

**Cromwell Road, SW7
Tel: 01-589 6371
01-581 4894 (Recorded Information)**

⊖ South Kensington

Many and varied collections including 19th century British painting and British sculpture. European and Oriental armour, furniture and decorative arts. Various temporary exhibitions throughout the year.

Open: Mon–Sat 10.00–17.50. Sun 14.30–17.50.
Voluntary admission charge.

P u ♿ Lifts. Wheelchairs on loan. Groups please notify in advance.

✗ Restaurants. School parties can arrange picnic facilities in Museum.

Combine with: Kensington Gardens, Natural History Museum, Science Museum.

Tower Bridge

WESTMINSTER ABBEY

Broad Sanctuary, SW1
Tel: 01-222 5152

⊖ Westminster

Shrine of St. Edward, burial place of Kings and Queens of England, scene of Coronations, resting place or memorial of many of our famous heroes, statesmen and poets, the Abbey is a 900-year living testimony to the faith of our mediaeval ancestors. Collection of wax and wooden effigies in Museum.

Nave and cloisters open daily 08.00–18.00 (20.00 Weds) **Free.** Royal Chapels, Poet's Corner, Choir and Statesmen's Aisle open Mon–Fri 09.00–16.45 (20.00 Weds), Sat 09.00–14.45 and 15.45–17.45. (Last admission 45 minutes before closing time.)
Admission charge. CD Under 16.

Chapter House, Treasury, Pyx Chamber and Undercroft Museum open daily 10.30–16.30.
Admission charge.

🅿 p ♿ Royal Chapels.

✗ Snack bars and restaurants nearby.

Combine with: Brass Rubbing Centre, Changing the Guard (Horse Guards Parade), Houses of Parliament, Cabinet War Rooms.

WHITBREAD STABLES

Garrett Street, EC1
Tel: 01-606 4455 ext. 2534

⇌ ⊖ Moorgate

⊖ Barbican (closed Sundays)

Working stables with 16 working Shire horses. See a farrier at work (mornings only). Show Harness room, wheelwright room with drays. Please give advance notice of visit by ringing telephone number above.

Open: Mon–Fri 11.00–12.30 and 13.30–15.00. Under 16 **Free.**

🅿 a ♿

Combine with: Barbican Centre, Museum of London.

WHITECHAPEL ART GALLERY

Whitechapel High Street, E1
Tel: 01-377 0107/5015

⊖ Aldgate East

Art gallery, housing temporary exhibitions of contemporary art. Also special workshop programmes for children, phone for details.

Open: Tue, Thur–Sun 11.00–17.00, Wed 11.00–20.00. Closed Mon. **Free.** (Adult admission charge for some exhibitions.) Bookshop.

♿ ✗

Combine with: Tower Bridge, Tower of London, Bethnal Green Museum of Childhood.

WINDSOR CASTLE

Windsor, Berkshire
Tel: (0753) 868286

⇌ Windsor and Eton Central and Riverside stations

Green Line Bus 700, 701, 702, 703

An 800 year old fortress situated in picturesque historic town. The areas of the castle open are: State apartments, St. George's Chapel, Queen Mary's Dolls' House, the Exhibition of Drawings and the Exhibition of The Queen's Presents and Royal Carriages. The Castle is the official residence of the Royal Family and the State apartments are closed when The Queen is in Official Residence. This is normally Easter, June and the latter part of December.

Opening times: The Castle precincts are open daily 10.00–16.15 approx (open later in spring and summer). State Apartments Mon–Sat 10.30–15.00 approx also some summer Sunday afternoons (open later in summer). For exact dates and times, please telephone Windsor (0753) 868286 or contact local Tourist Office.
Admission charge to all exhibitions, the State Apartments and St. George's Chapel. CD Under 16. Precincts **Free.**

🅿 Goswell Road, Windsor.

♿ Wheelchairs are admitted to State apartments at the discretion of the Head Warden. It is not advisable to expect entry on Sunday afternoons or at other peak times.

✗ Restaurants and cafes in Windsor.

Combine with: Royalty and Empire Exhibition, Windsor Safari Park.

PARKS

BATTERSEA PARK, SW11

Tel: 01-871 7530

≋ Battersea Park

⊖ Sloane Square then bus 19, 137

A riverside park (200 acres) with a boating lake (Easter–Oct) fishing and water fowl, Deer enclosure, children's zoo with pony rides (Good Friday–end of Oct) play park, one-o'clock club, paddling pool, tennis courts, athletics track with fitness circuit, cricket nets. Children's shows, band concerts and other entertainments throughout the summer. Disabled persons garden and WC's, old English garden, heather and herb gardens and alpine and show house, Japanese Peace Pagoda. **Free.**

🅿 🚐 on site ♿ 🚾 ✕ Lakeside cafeteria, picnicking in the park.

Combine with: National Army Museum, Tate Gallery.

BROCKWELL PARK, SE24

Tel: 01-674 6141

≋ Herne Hill/Brixton

⊖ Brixton

Summer play schemes for children, sports facilities including swimming and tennis. Concerts, music, one-o'clock club, playground, gardens, paddling pool (April–Oct) aviary. **Free.**

♿ Cafe in old Mansion House.

BURGESS PARK, SE5

Tel: 01-703 3911

≋ ⊖ Elephant and Castle

Newly created park. Facilities include a lake with sailing dinghies and canoes for hire. Trained instructors available for tuition in sailing and canoeing. Fishing. Play park, one-o'clock club (check open days) large children's playground with paddling pool, glasshouse and small multi-gym. Polygrass pitch for 5-a-side, hockey and football (must be pre-booked), Go-Kart track. Two information centres show the development of the park and local ecology. Natural areas. **Free.**

CRYSTAL PALACE PARK, SE20

Tel: 01-778 7148

≋ Crystal Palace

200 acre park with boating lake, fishing and water fowl. Large size models of pre-historic animals on an island in the lake. Children's zoo (Good Friday–end Sept). **Admission charge.** Pony and pony and trap rides, animal and bird enclosures, play park, one-o'clock club. **Free.** Children's shows in the summer, open-air concert bowl. The terraces of the former Crystal Palace Exhibition Centre are being restored but are not open to the public.

Children's funfair (March–Oct depending on weather), visiting circus and steam fair (check for dates).

The National Sports Centre (01-778 0131) venue of international and national athletics and many other sports has many facilities including an artificial ski-slope (open Oct–March).

🅿 🚐 on site ✕ Cafeteria (March–Oct) picnicking in the park.

Combine with: Horniman Museum, Dulwich Picture Gallery.

FINSBURY PARK, N4

Tel: 01-263 5001

≋ Finsbury Park

⊖ Finsbury Park/Manor House

Dating from 1869 this was London's first planned municipal park. Children's shows during the summer holidays. One-o'clock club, playpark (Easter–August only) and children's playground. Athletics track, boating lake, fishing and other sports facilities – summer coaching programme in various sports, Mon–Fri. **Free.**

🅿 Limited public parking ♿ 🚾

✕ Cafeteria open March–Oct.

HAMPSTEAD AND THE HEATH

**Golders Hill,
West Heath and Sandy Heath
Tel: 01-455 5183**

**Parliament Hill, East Heath
and Kenwood   Tel: 01-485 4491**

≥ Gospel Oak/Hampstead Heath

⊖ Hampstead

More than 800 acres of heath and woodland. The facilities for children include Whitestone Pond, where model boats are sailed (off North End Way) and to the north west is Golders Hill which has a flower garden and a wide variety of animal life including a deer enclosure. Parliament Hill has an athletics track, paddling pool (summer only), play park, adventure playground for the over 12's, one-o'clock club and lido (open May–Sept approx.).

Free fishing is allowed in the 2 ponds on the Hampstead side and 2 on the Highgate side of the Heath, except during the closed season March–June.

During the summer, there are special children's shows and on Bank Holidays there are two fairs, one off East Heath Road and the other off Spaniards Road. For further information telephone LTB's Information Service on 01-730 3488, a few days before the Bank Holiday. **Free.**

Open-air concerts take place during the summer months at the Kenwood Concert Bowl.

P off East Heath Road and off Hampstead Lane.

&. **wc** at Parliament Hill (by entrance to athletics track).

✗ Cafeterias at Parliament Hill and Golders Hill (March–Oct). Numerous restaurants in Hampstead Village.

HYDE PARK, W2

Tel: 01-262 5484

⊖ Hyde Park Corner/Marble Arch

The Serpentine has a lido with a children's paddling pool and sandpit. (Open May–Sept). Rowing boats, skiffs, canoes and motor boats are available for hire (March–Oct). Wildlife includes swans and geese. Band concerts take place on Sundays (May–Aug).

There is a putting green and four tennis courts near Knightsbridge Barracks. Fishing in the Serpentine is allowed if you

have a licence. To apply for a licence, write to: The Superintendent's Office, The Store Yard, Hyde Park, London, W2.

P v j &. ✗ Serpentine Restaurant and Pagoda Restaurant.

To the west of Hyde Park is:

KENSINGTON GARDENS, W2

Tel: 01-937 4848

⊖ Queensway/Lancaster Gate/High Street Kensington

In the north-west section of Kensington Gardens, near Queensway Underground station, there is a children's playground and nearby is the Elfin Oak – a tree with lots of carvings of animals and birds around it. In August, children's puppet shows are held near here. There is another small playground near Lancaster Gate Underground station. To the south is the Round Pond where people sail model boats or nearby, fly kites. There are many species of waterfowl to be found by the Long Water and the famous statue of Peter Pan is on its western bank. **Free.**

P v j &. ✗ Restaurants, snack bars and cafes in Bayswater, Knightsbridge and Kensington.

Combine with: Commonwealth Institute, Kensington Palace, London Toy and Model Museum, Queens Ice Skating Rink, Science Museum, Victoria and Albert Museum.

REGENT'S PARK, NW1

Tel: 01-486 7905

⊖ Regent's Park/Camden Town, then bus 74

Perhaps the prettiest of the Royal Parks and always full of flowers. Four children's playgrounds with attendants at Hanover Gate, Primrose Hill, Marylebone Green and Gloucester Gate. Children's pond with canoes at Hanover Gate. Rowing boats can be hired in the lake (March–Oct – check for availability on 01-486 4759). Tennis courts, cricket, rounders, softball (during summer), hockey, rugby and football pitches (during winter) can be booked. Military band concerts take place in the summer and there are puppet shows for children from the end of July–August. Open-air theatre performances take place in summer. Art Gallery. Park open daily 07.00–dusk. **Free.**

P 🚐 on site at Gloucester slips near Zoo.

&. ✗ Picnicking, restaurants.

Combine with: London Zoo, Madame Tussaud's, Planetarium.

RICHMOND PARK

Richmond, Surrey
Tel: 01-948 3209

≋ Richmond, then bus 65, 71

⊖ Richmond, then bus 65, 71

Red and Fallow Deer roam freely in lots of open parkland. Ideal for picnics. Childrens playground at Richmond end of park (near Petersham Road).

🅿 on site 🚌 Single deck coaches only. Mon–Fri Permits from the Superintendent's Office.

✗ Restaurants on Richmond and Roehampton sides of park.

Combine with: Kew Bridge Steam Museum, Royal Botanic Gardens, Kew.

ROYAL BOTANIC GARDENS

Kew, Richmond, Surrey
Tel: 01-940 1171

≋ Kew Gardens

⊖ Kew Gardens

Boat from Westminster Pier (summer only)

300 acres of garden with over 25,000 plant species. Hothouses, see also the recently opened "Princess of Wales" conservatory. Museum of useful plants, wood museum. Quiz sheets. Guided tours for groups of children over 7 years.
Admission charge. Under 10's **Free.**

Kew Palace, Queen's Cottage Gardens Open: daily (except 25 Dec and 1 Jan) 09.30–16.00/20.00 (according to season).

Kew Palace Open: daily (April–Sept) 11.00–17.30, Cottage Open: Sat and Sun (April–Sept) 11.00–17.30.
Admission charge. 🆑 Under 16.

🅿 Kew Green/Queen Elizabeth's Lawn.

🚌 Kew Lawn (space permitting).

♿ Wheelchairs for hire at Main Gate. Please notify in advance.

✗ Tea Bar. Refreshment Pavilion (summer only).

Combine with: Kew Bridge Steam Museum, Syon House and Park.

ST.JAMES'S PARK, SW1

Tel: 01-930 1793

⊖ Victoria/St. James's Park/Charing Cross

Very popular and attractive gardens near Buckingham Palace. The large lake is home for pelicans and many kinds of ducks. Childrens' playground. Military band concerts in the summer. **Free.**

🅿 q ♿ 🆆🅲 at Marlborough Gate.

✗ Cafeteria and snack bar.

Combine with: Cabinet War Rooms, Changing the Guard, Houses of Parliament, Westminster Abbey.

VICTORIA PARK, E2

Tel: 01-985 1957

≋ Cambridge Heath/Hackney Wick

⊖ Mile End, then bus

⊖ Bethnal Green, then bus

One of London's oldest parks bordering on the Regent's Canal. It has a playpark (Easter–Aug), one-o'clock club and a children's playground. Animal enclosure and mobile zoo visits. model boating and fishing, athletics track and lido. Children's shows in the summer. May festival and visiting fairs.

🚌 ♿ 🆆🅲 ✗ Refreshments at boating lake all year.

Combine with: Bethnal Green Museum of Childhood.

Kew Gardens

FARM VISITS

Community City Farm,
232 Grafton Road, NW5
Tel: 01-482 2861

≥ Kentish Town West

≥ ⊖ Kentish Town

Open: daily 09.30–18.00 summer, 09.30–17.30 winter.

Cows, sheep, pigs, goats, ducks and chickens.

Elm Farm,
Gladstone Terrace,
(off Lockington Road), SW8
Tel: 01-627 1130

≥ Battersea Park/Queenstown Road

Open: Tues–Thurs, Sat and Sun 08.30–17.00.

Goats, cows, sheep, rabbits, chickens. Natural pond area. Cafe.

Freightliners Farm,
Paradise Park,
Sheringham Road, N7
Tel: 01-609 0467

⊖ Holloway Road/Highbury and Islington

Open: Tues–Sun 11.00–13.00 and 14.00–17.00.

Cattle, sheep, goats, poultry, pony and donkey, dogs and cats.

Kentish Town City Farm,
1 Cressfield Close,
(off Grafton Road), NW5
Tel: 01-482 2861

≥ Gospel Oak

≥ ⊖ Kentish Town

Open: daily 09.00–17.30. **Free.** Donations welcome.

Mudchute Farm,
Pier Street,
(off Manchester Road), SE11
Tel: 01-515 5901

⊖ Mile End then bus 277

DLR Mudchute

Open: Mon–Sun 09.00–17.00

Sheep, cattle, goats, chicken and rabbits.

**Park Lodge Farm,
Harvil Road, Harefield, Uxbridge,
Middlesex
Tel: (089582) 4425**

⊖ Uxbridge, then bus (infrequent)

530 acre dairy and sheep farm (school and college parties only). Occasionally open weekends. See press for details.

**Spitalfields Farm Association,
c/o Thomas Buxton Junior School,
Buxton Street,
(main entrance Weaver Street), E1
Tel: 01-247 8762**

⊖ Whitechapel/Aldgate East/Shoreditch (peak hours only)

Open: daily 09.00–18.30, closed Mondays. **Free.**

&

**Stepney Stepping Stones Farm,
Stepney Way, E1
Tel: 01-790 8204**

⇌ / DLR Limehouse

⊖ Stepney Green

Open: Tues–Sun 09.30–18.00 also open all Bank Holiday Mondays. (Closed 13.00–14.00). **Free.** Donations welcome. Groups and coach parties should book in advance.

&

**Surrey Docks Farm,
Rotherhithe Street,
Rotherhithe, SE16
Tel: 01-231 1010**

⊖ Surrey Docks

Open: Tues–Sun 10.00–17.00. Closed 13.00–14.00 at weekends and during school holidays and Fri during school holidays. **Free.** Donations welcomed.

**Vauxhall City Farm,
Tyers Street,
(off Kensington Lane), SE11
Tel: 01-582 4204**

⇌ ⊖ Vauxhall

Open: Tues–Thurs, Sat and Sun 10.30–17.00.

Cows, sheep, goats, ducks and chickens.

NATURE TRAILS

A fun way to explore our many parks is to follow a nature trail. Most London boroughs have specially created nature trails with information leaflets to accompany them to help you get the most out of your visit. For further information contact the relevant London Borough information service (address and tel. nos. on back cover).

**Dulwich Park, Southwark, SE21
Tel: 01-693 5737**

The Tree Trail highlights the varied tree species to be found in the park. A booklet on the Trail is available from the Park Manager's Officer for a small charge.

**Horniman Gardens,
Forest Hill, SE23
Tel: 01-699 8924**

Three separate walks: The Coach Trail, The Dutch Barn Trail and The Railway Trail, which follows the track of the old Crystal Palace high level railway line. Two guides to the Trails are available from the Park Manager's Office and the Horniman Museum for a nominal fee.

**Trent Park
Tel: 01-449 8706**

Popular nature trail, Pets Corner. Groups advised to contact the Park Manager prior to their visit. Guided walks for groups, also by prior arrangement. Special three quarter mile woodland trail for the visually handicapped.

**Passmore Edwards Nature
Reserve, Norman Road, E6
Tel: 01-470 4525**

⊖ East Ham then Bus 101 or S1

Nine acre churchyard divided into several habitat areas with marked nature trail, Interpretive Centre and exhibition on natural history.

Display room open: Tues, Thurs, Sat and Sun 14.00–17.00. Grounds open: Mon–Fri 09.00–17.00 summer, open weekends only in winter 14.00–17.00.

ZOOS AND SAFARI PARKS

CHESSINGTON WORLD OF ADVENTURES

Leatherhead Road, Chessington, Surrey
Tel: (03727) 27227

≇ Chessington South (10 minutes walk from attraction)

New pay-one-price family adventure attractions featuring six themed areas with four major new rides: Calamity Canyon and the Runaway Mine Train, The Mystic East and Dragon River, Journey into the Fifth Dimension, Zoological Gardens – wild animals from all over the world plus Safari Skyway, Circus World including the Circus Academy and the English Village. Other facilities include Mother and Baby Room, and gift shops.

Open: daily except 25 Dec, April–Oct 10.00–17.00 (All attractions), Nov–March 10.00–16.00 (Zoological Gardens only).
Admission charge. Under 4's **Free.**
CD 14 and under.
P 🚐 Free ሀ ✗ Restaurants, refreshments, bar.

LONDON ZOO

Regent's Park, NW1
Tel: 01-722 3333

⊖ Camden Town/Baker Street then bus 74. Bus Z1 (summer only) Oxford Circus/Baker Street to London Zoo.

All kinds of mammals, birds, reptiles, fishes and insects. See the rare Giant Panda and meet the young elephants out walking. Junior and Family Friends of the Zoo scheme with season ticket, newsletters, special events. Talks arranged for school parties. Pushchairs for hire. Mother and Baby room. In summer there are daily "Meet the Animals" shows in the Hummingbird Amphitheatre, and animal rides.

Open: daily (except 25 Dec) 09.00–18.00 (summer), 10.00–16.00 (winter).
Admission charge. Under 5's **Free.**
CD Under 16.
P 🚐 in Regent's Park car park ሀ

✗ Large cafeteria, restaurant and cafes, picnicking. Packed lunches can be eaten in the covered Humming Bird Amphitheatre.

WHIPSNADE PARK ZOO

Dunstable, Bedfordshire
Tel: (0582) 872171

≇ Luton, then bus from Luton to Dunstable (many services from bus station), then bus 43 Dunstable to Whipsnade Park Zoo (stops outside gates).

Green Line Bus: 937 from Victoria (Eccleston Bridge) Sundays and Public Holidays SUMMER ONLY.

All kinds of animals roaming in open-air enclosures. Railway, Dolphinarium, Children's Zoo with baby penguin rearing unit. Free flying bird displays given by the Birds of Prey and Falconry Centre of Newent daily (except Fridays). New Discovery Centre.

Open: Mon–Sat 10.00–18.00, Sun and Bank Holidays 10.00–19.00 (or sunset if earlier).
Admission charge. Under 5's **Free.**
CD Under 15. Season ticket.
P 🚐 on site ሀ Wheelchairs (and pushchairs) for hire.

✗ Self-service cafeteria, picnicking – picnic shelters all round the park, also Tea Bar and shelter on the Downs.

WINDSOR SAFARI PARK

Winkfield Road, Windsor, Berkshire
Tel: (0753) 869841

≇ Windsor and Eton Central and Riverside stations, then local bus.

Green Line bus 700 direct from Victoria (Eccleston Bridge) summer only. Other times, Green Line bus 701/702/703 then local bus.

From the safety of your car or coach see lions, tigers, giraffes, llamas, camels baboons, rhinos, elephants and many more animals roaming free. Don't miss feeding time! See the famous killer whale, dolphin and sealion show, see the parrot and birds of prey show (summer only) also computer animated "Tiki" show and the "Tropical World" of plants, alligators and butterflies.

Open: daily (except 25 Dec) from 10.00 until an hour before dusk.
Admission charge – includes entry to all shows, "Tiki" show, "Tropical World" and all children's play centres. Under 4's **Free.**
CD Under 15.
P 🚐 on site ሀ all facilities.

✗ Restaurant, cafeteria and picnic areas (various picnic areas including covered picnic area in Parrot House).

Combine with: Windsor Castle, Royalty and Empire.

CRICKET

**Cricket Memorial Gallery,
Lord's Cricket Ground, NW8
Tel: 01-289 1611**

⊖ St. John's Wood

The MCC's collection of paintings and cricketana. Open: (on match days) Mon–Sat 10.30–17.00. Admission on all other days with conducted tours by prior arrangement with the curator.
Admission charge. CD Under 16.

School parties are admitted free if arranged in advance (except at weekends).

P on site & Please contact gallery in advance.

✕ Refreshments available on match days.

Combine with: London Zoo, Madame Tussauds, Planetarium.

During the summer, international county and youth matches are played at:

**Lord's Cricket Ground,
St. John's Wood Road, NW8
Tel: 01-286 8011 (prospect of play)
01-289 1615 (other enquiries)**

⊖ St. John's Wood

**Oval Cricket Ground,
Kennington Oval, SE11
Tel: 01-582 6660**

⊖ Oval
& ✕

FOOTBALL

and other sports

**Wembley Stadium,
Wembley, Middlesex** 🅛
Tel: 01-903 4864

⊖ Wembley Park

Guided tours of London's largest sports stadium. Visit the players' changing rooms, trophy cabinet and Royal Box; you can also walk up to the Players' Tunnel accompanied by the sound of the spectators. Short audio-visual presentation depicting the history of the stadium and the first Wembley Cup Final. Gift shop.

Tours: Daily at 10.00, 11.00, 12.00, 13.00, 14.00, 15.00, 16.00 (16.00 tour summer only). No tours 25 and 26 Dec and 1 Jan or the day of an event.

P 🚌 on site & limited ✕ nearby.

The Oval

HORSE RIDING

Enjoy a ride in Hyde Park on the 2½ mile riding track. It is best to book in advance as this is a very popular pastime. Tuition is available. Contact:

**Bathurst Riding Stables,
63 Bathurst Mews, W2
Tel: 01-723 2813**

⊖ Paddington/Lancaster Gate

Minimum age 7.

**Ross Nye's Riding Establishment,
8 Bathurst Mews, W2
Tel: 01-262 3791**

⊖ Paddington/Lancaster Gate

Minimum age 8 (closed July and August).

**Lilo Blum,
32a Grosvenor Crescent Mews, SW1
Tel: 01-235 6846**

⊖ Hyde Park Corner

Ponies available for very young children – minimum age approx 2 years.

ICE SKATING

There are several ice-skating rinks in London. Boots are available for hire. **Admission charge.**

**Lee Valley Ice Centre,
Lea Bridge Road, Leyton, E10
Tel: 01-533 3151**

⇌ Clapton, then long walk

Buses 38, 48, 55, 52

**Michael Sobell Sports Centre,
Hornsey Road, N7
Tel: 01-607 1632**

⇌ ⊖ Finsbury Park

**Queens Ice Skating Club,
Queensway, W2
Tel: 01-229 0172**

⊖ Queensway/Bayswater

**Richmond Ice Rink,
Clevedon Road,
(by Richmond Bridge),
Twickenham, Middlesex
Tel: 01-892 3646**

⇌ ⊖ Richmond

**Romford Ice Rink,
Rom Valley Way,
Romford, Essex
Tel: (0708) 24731**

≊ Romford, then short walk

**Streatham Ice Rink,
386 Streatham High Road, SW16
Tel: 01-769 7771**

≊ Streatham/Streatham Common

ROLLER SKATING

You can roller skate at the following rinks. Skates available for hire. Day and evening sessions.

**Finsbury Leisure Centre,
Norman Street, EC1
Tel: 01-253 4490**

≊ ⊖ Old Street

**Harrow Leisure Centre,
Christchurch Avenue,
Harrow, Middlesex
Tel: 01-863 5611 Ext. 2724**

≊ ⊖ Harrow & Wealdstone

**Picketts Lock Sports Centre,
Picketts Lock Lane, Edmonton, N9
Tel: 01-803 4756**

≊ Lower Edmonton, then bus W8

OUTDOORS
**Battersea Park, SW11
Tel: 01-871 7530**

≊ Battersea Park

⊖ Sloane Square, then bus 19, 137

Tarmac areas, near athletics track, available for use when space not required for other park event. (Skates not available for hire.)

SPORTS CENTRES

London's many sports centres have all kinds of sporting activities for children and tuition is usually available. Here are some of the major sporting centres:

**Brixton Recreation Centre,
Brixton Station Road, SW9
Tel: 01-274 7774**

≊ ⊖ Brixton

Summer activity programmes available to children who apply for "Outreach" summer activity programme card.

**Crystal Palace National Sports
Centre, Norwood, SE19
Tel: 01-778 0131**

≊ Crystal Palace

Special summer and Easter holiday programmes (book in advance).

**Elephant and Castle Recreation
Centre, 22 Elephant and Castle, SE1
Tel: 01-582 5505**

≊ ⊖ Elephant and Castle

Children's coaching in most sports including trampolining.

**Finsbury Leisure Centre,
Norman Street, EC1
Tel: 01-253 4490**

≊ ⊖ Old Street

Summer activity programme, Junior programme on Saturdays for rest of year. Sports include trampolining, judo and badminton.

**Harrow Leisure Centre,
Christchurch Avenue,
Harrow, Middlesex
Tel: 01-863 5611 Ext. 2724**

≊ ⊖ Harrow and Wealdstone

Children's recreation programme during school holidays. Sports include badminton, squash, football, table tennis and short tennis. At other times, tuition given in swimming, junior judo, short tennis and football.

**Michael Sobell Sports Centre,
Hornsey Road, Islington, N7
Tel: 01-607 1632**

≊ ⊖ Finsbury Park

Special summer session times for children, sports include badminton, ice-skating and tennis. Additionally, all year, judo, karate, trampolining and inflatables.

**Picketts Lock Centre,
Picketts Lock Lane, N9
Tel: 01-803 4756**

≊ Lower Edmonton then bus W8

Summer holiday activities for children include multisports sessions, ice-skating, swimming and inflatables.

SPORT

**Peckham Leisure Centre,
McKerrell Road, SE15
Tel: 01-732 3516**

⇌ Queens Road, Peckham/Peckham Rye

Supervised play sessions for under 5's, indoor athletics for under 16's, Tai boxing, badminton, judo, gymnastics and basketball.

**Queen Mother Sports Centre,
223 Vauxhall Bridge Road, SW1
Tel: 01-798 2125 (General Enquiries)
01-834 4726 (Bookings)**

⇌ ⊖ Victoria

Summer programme of activities including trampolining, badminton, squash, short tennis, table tennis, abseiling, canoeing and judo.

SWIMMING

Most of the sports centres listed on page 41 have swimming pools The following centres have wave machines (and/or waterchutes):

**Clapton Pools,
39 Lower Clapton Road, E5
Tel: 01-985 0961/2158**

⇌ Clapton

Water-ski machine operational all year, special session times. (No wave machine.)

**The Dolphin Centre,
Main Road, Romford, Essex
Tel: (0708) 751525**

⇌ Romford

**Elephant and Castle Leisure Pool,
22 Elephant and Castle, SE1
Tel: 01-582 5505**

⇌ ⊖ Elephant and Castle

Elephant slide.

**Eltham Swimming Pool,
Eltham Hill, SE9
Tel: 01-850 4756**

⇌ Eltham

100 feet long "Supachute". (No wave machine.)

**The Fulham Pools,
Normand Park, Lillie Road, SW6
Tel: 01-385 7628**

⊖ West Brompton

Waterslide.

**The Kingfisher,
Fairfield Road,
Kingston-upon-Thames, Surrey
Tel: 01-546 1042**

⇌ Kingston

**Latchmere Leisure Pool,
Latchmere Road, Battersea, SW11
Tel: 01-871 7470**

⇌ Clapham Junction

**The Big Splash,
(Open-air swimming pool),
Mapleton Road, SW18
Tel: 01-870 4955**

⇌ Wandsworth Town, then bus

⊖ East Putney, then bus

2 waterchutes, inflatables, "Bubble Tub". (No wave machine.)

**White City Pool,
Bloemfontein Road, W12
Tel: 01-743 3401**

⊖ Shepherds Bush

Waterchutes, beaching area, cafe.

**Wild Waters,
Old Deer Park, Richmond, Surrey
Tel: 01-940 9966**

⇌ ⊖ Richmond

4 waterslides. (No wave machine.)

TENNIS

**Wimbledon Lawn Tennis Museum,
The All England Club,
Church Road, SW19
Tel: 01-946 6131**

⇌ ⊖ Wimbledon, then long walk

⇌ ⊖ Southfields, then walk

History of Lawn Tennis to date. Reconstructions, equipment, fashion, listening posts, films, library and view over the Centre Court. Open: Tues–Sat 11.00–17.00, Sun 14.00–17.00 (during the annual Tennis Championships, the museum is open to those with tickets to the grounds only). **Admission charge.** Under 16.

P on site Restaurants and snack bars in Wimbledon Village.

CINEMAS

The following cinemas show special films for children. Check for details before setting off.

**Barbican Cinema,
Barbican Centre, Silk Street, EC2
Tel: 01-628 8795/01-638 8891**

≥≥ ⊖ Moorgate

⊖ Barbican (closed Sundays)/St. Paul's

**Battersea Arts Centre,
Old Town Hall, Lavender Hill, SW11
Tel: 01-223 8413**

≥≥ Clapham Junction

**ICA, Nash House,
The Mall, SW1
Tel: 01-930 3647**

≥≥ ⊖ Charing Cross

⊖ Piccadilly Circus

**National Film Theatre,
South Bank, SE1
Tel: 01-928 3232**

≥≥ ⊖ Waterloo

**Rio Centre,
107 Kingsland High Street, E8
Tel: 01-254 6677**

≥≥ Dalston Kingsland

Matinees for children during summer, Saturday morning shows during winter.

CIRCUSES

There are no permanent circuses in London, the nearest is at Chessington World of Adventures (See p 38). There are normally other circuses in London during Bank Holiday weekends and at Christmas. For details of venues, phone the LTB Information Service on 01-730 3488, nearer the time.

FUNFAIRS

There are usually funfairs at Alexandra Palace, Blackheath, Finsbury Park and Hampstead Heath at Easter, spring and summer Bank Holidays. For further information please phone LTB Information Service open 01-730 3488 nearer the time.

THEATRES

BARBICAN CENTRE

Silk Street, EC2
Tel: 01-638 4141 Ext. 218/365

≋ ⊖ Moorgate

⊖ Barbican (closed Sundays), St. Paul's

Annual family festival during the summer holiday. Children's concerts and activities during the holidays. Children's cinema club every Saturday. Home of Royal Shakespeare Company.

🅿 on site ♿ ✘ Restaurant on site.

Combine with: Museum of London.

BATTERSEA ARTS CENTRE

Old Town Hall, Lavender Hill, SW11
Tel: 01-223 2223

≋ Clapham Junction

Children's shows every Sunday afternoon.

Arrangements can be made for space to eat packed lunches by contacting the Box Office in advance.

JACKSON'S LANE COMMUNITY CENTRE

Archway Road, N6
Tel: 01-340 5226

⊖ Highgate

Children's shows during holidays.

✘ Cafe.

LITTLE ANGEL MARIONETTE THEATRE

14 Dagmar Passage, Cross Street, N1
(Dagmar Passage is not marked on maps. Look for Dagmar Terrace)
Tel: 01-226 1787

≋ Highbury and Islington

⊖ Angel/Highbury and Islington

London's famous puppet theatre is a centre of creative endeavour visited by enthusiasts from every part of the world. Performances on Sat and Sun at 15.00 and during the week in the holidays. Plays for very young children take place on Sat mornings at 11.00. Bookings accepted by telephone.

🅿 Meter parking nearby ♿

✘ Coffee bar serving soft drinks and snacks, snack bars nearby.

THE LONDON BUBBLE

A Mobile Arts Company
Office address:
5 Elephant Lane, SE16
Tel: 01-237 4434

Shows, events, workshops and participatory projects – with the accent on excitement – all over London, all year round. Phone for details of the summer "Tent" tour which travels through London's parks from May–Sept each year.

LYRIC THEATRE, HAMMERSMITH

King Street, Hammersmith, W6
Tel: 01-741 2311

⊖ Hammersmith

Children's show every Saturday at 11.00 and every Sunday at 12.00. All tickets £1.00. Children's lunches available at the weekend with special "Clown service" on Sundays between 12.00 and 14.30. Free Foyer Music Sat and Sun. Advance booking recommended for all activities.

🅿 🚐 ✕ ♿

MOLECULE THEATRE OF SCIENCE FOR CHILDREN

Bloomsbury Theatre,
15 Gordon Street, WC1
Tel: 01-388 5739

⇌ Euston

⊖ Euston/Euston Square

Scientific adventure plays for children from 7-11 years and also "Molecule Discussions" which are given by eminent scientists for 13-18 year olds.

Performances take place in September and January each year (phone for details).

🅿 n g ♿ ✕ Coffee Bar

POLKA CHILDREN'S THEATRE

240 The Broadway, SW19
Tel: 01-543 4888/01-543 0363

⇌ Wimbledon

⊖ Wimbledon/South Wimbledon

Children's theatre performances. Exhibitions of "Puppets of the World", "Toys of Britain" and art in "Link Picture Gallery", workshops, puppet and music classes, drama, mime and dance. Toyshop and playground.

Open: Tues–Fri 10.00–16.30, Sat 12.00–18.30. Performances morning and afternoon.
Admission to building and exhibitions **Free.** Enquire at Box Office for show prices and times.

🅿 Street parking ♿

✕ Snacks in the Polka Pantry. Birthday teas can be arranged. By pre-arrangement, school parties may eat packed lunches in the "Link Picture Gallery" and "Adventure Room".

Combine with: Wimbledon Lawn Tennis Museum.

PUPPET THEATRE BARGE

Box Office:
78 Middleton Road, E8
Tel: 01-249 6876

⊖ Camden Town (for barge itself)

A marionette theatre on a converted Thames barge, the company is based at: Camden Lock, 289 Camden High Street, NW1, Oct–April.

During the summer months, the company tours the canals and the river Thames, performing at various venues en route. Performances for adults and children take place on Sat and Sun throughout the year and daily during the holidays. Other times by prior arrangement. Advance bookings can be made by phone.

SOUTH BANK CENTRE

Belvedere Road, SE1
Tel: 01-928 3002
(General Information)
≋ ⊖ Waterloo

The Centre comprises 3 concert halls (Royal Festival Hall, Queen Elizabeth Hall and Purcell Room – Box Office: 01-928 3191), the National Film Theatre, the National Theatre, Hayward Art Gallery and Craft Centre. Book shops, record shop. Adjacent to the centre is Jubilee Gardens.

Regular Saturday morning arts workshops during term time for 7-12 year olds, children's concerts, free exhibitions, lunchtime music in the Royal Festival Hall. Annual events include "Thamesday" and "Children's Day" (for dates see list of MAJOR EVENTS FOR CHILDREN on page 49).

P ⊞ ☖ WC in Royal Festival Hall and Jubilee Gardens.

✗ Buffet and cafeteria in Royal Festival Hall and National Theatre and National Film Theatre.

TRICYCLE THEATRE

269 Kilburn High Road, NW6
Tel: 01-328 8626
≋ Brondesbury
⊖ Kilburn

Although damaged by a fire this year (1987), the Tricycle Theatre still organises activities for children aged 3-12 years such as workshops in music, drama and clowning skills. Children's shows take place on Saturdays. Please phone for details. The rebuilt Tricycle Theatre is due to open in Sept 1988.

UNICORN THEATRE FOR CHILDREN

6 Great Newport Street, WC2
Tel: 01-836 3334
⊖ Leicester Square

A variety of plays and children's shows suitable for 4-12 year olds. Performances for the general public take place on weekend afternoons and there are schools performances mid-week. Details of club activities and schools performances can be obtained by writing or phoning the theatre.

Performances: General Sat and Sun 14.30, Schools Tues–Fri 14.00.
Admission charge.

P k ☖ ✗ Green Room snack bar – snacks, lunch and supper.

UPSTREAM CHILDREN'S THEATRE

St. Andrew's Church,
Short Street, SE1
Tel: 01-633 9819
≋ ⊖ Waterloo

Children's theatre workshop for 4-12 year olds on Saturdays and Wednesdays. Occasional performances. Phone for full details.

WAREHOUSE THEATRE, CROYDON

62 Dingwall Road, Croydon
Tel: 01-680 4060
≋ East Croydon

Children's shows every Saturday morning (no shows in August).

✗ Bar/Restaurant.

THE YOUNG VIC

66 The Cut, SE1
Tel: 01-633 0133 (Administration)
01-928 6363 (Box Office)
≋ ⊖ Waterloo

Plays and occasional workshops in the Main House and the Young Vic Studio. Wide-ranging repertoire with plays suitable for children aged 5-11 years and 11-18 years and over.

Shows for younger children 10.30, 14.00 and 19.00; other shows 19.30 with matinees – Times may vary. Half-price concessions bookable in advance. Special child rates for children's shows.

P d ☖ some facilities, please advise Box Office of visit.

✗ Cafe serving tea, snacks and hot and cold meals (including vegetarian) Open: Mon–Fri from 10.30 and on evenings and at weekends when there is a performance.

Burgers, pizzas and pasta dishes find favour with most children. Wimpy Hamburger Restaurants are long established and have many branches throughout London – some of the larger restaurants can provide a fun venue for children's parties so ask at your nearest Wimpy. Spaghetti House Restaurants also have many branches in London where, in the best Italian tradition, children are most welcome – most provide booster seats and smaller children's portions on request.

Here are a few more suggestions for places to eat out with children:

RESTAURANTS

Biguns,
122 Victoria Street, SW1
Tel: 01-630 5733

Included on the American style menu are ribs and burgers. Children's menu available for children up to 10 years. Open Sun.

Cafe Pelican,
45 St. Martin's Lane, WC2
Tel: 01-379 0309

French Brasserie-style restaurant with wide-ranging menu. Reduced price for children. Award from "Children's Welcome" guide 1986. Open Sun.

Eats and Treats,
188-196 Regent Street, W1
Tel: 01-734 3161

New coffee shop on lower ground floor of world famous Hamley's toy store. Menu includes hot and cold snacks, cakes and ice-creams. Plenty of space for prams, push-chairs and shopping. Late night opening Thurs.

Geales Fish Restaurant,
2 Farmer Street, W8
Tel: 01-727 7969

For many this is the best fish and chip shop in London. Highchairs and booster seats. Closed Sun and Mon.

Grandma Lee's,
2 Bridge Street, SW1
Tel: 01-839 1319

Restaurant and bakery open for breakfast, lunch and dinner. Highchairs available.

Lyons Corner House,
The Strand, WC2
Tel: 01-930 9381

Fast and reasonably priced British food. "Children's choice" menu for under 12 year olds. Highchairs and booster seats. Open Sun.

Magic Moments Restaurant,
233 Regent Street, W1
Tel: 01-499 6176

Fun venue for children. See magic performed at your table at lunchtime (Saturdays and Sundays only – minimum age 5 years). Children's menu and booster seats available.

Pizza Express,
29 Wardour Street, W1
Tel: 01-437 7215

London's original Pizza restaurant, many branches throughout London. Highchairs. Open Sun.

Quality Inns,
191 Victoria Street, SW1
Tel: 01-834 0206

Restaurant offering International menu with several other central London branches. Children's menu and highchairs. Open Sun.

Rock Garden,
6-7 The Piazza,
Covent Garden, WC2
Tel: 01-836 4052

Varied menu including the ever popular hamburgers. Here they make them in 3 sizes. Centrally placed restaurant famed for evening rock band performances. Open Sun.

Smollensky's Balloon Restaurant,
1 Dover Street, W1
Tel: 01-491 1199

American style restaurant offering baby-sitting service on Sat and Sun afternoons. (NOT during school holidays.) Parents and children can enjoy a meal together (children's menu and highchairs available) and afterwards, an entertainer keeps the children occupied from 12.30–15.00 giving parents the chance to enjoy a little sight-seeing or shopping on their own until approx 17.00.

WHERE TO EAT PACKED LUNCHES UNDER COVER

When the weather is fine, nothing could be nicer than to have a picnic in one of our many parks or in the grounds of a London attraction. Do not despair if the weather is not so good, as the following places provide areas under cover where you can eat a packed lunch – (some places can only provide this facility for groups).

Battersea Arts Centre
HMS Belfast – (groups)
British Museum
Chislehurst Caves
Imperial War Museum
London Dungeon – (groups)
London Transport Museum
London Zoo
Mountfitchet Castle
Museum of London
National Army Museum
Polka Children's Theatre – (groups)
RAF Museum
Tower of London
Victoria and Albert Museum – (groups)
Whipsnade Park Zoo
Windsor Safari Park

DISCOTHEQUE

Le Beat Route,
16-17 Greek Street, W1
Tel: 01-734 6308/437 5782

Under 18 discotheque Tues and Wed 19.00–23.00, Sun 19.30–24.00. Entrance fee. Soft drinks only.

P g

Natural History Museum

MAJOR EVENTS FOR CHILDREN

January
Charles I Commemoration
– Whitehall, SW1
London International Boat Show
– Earls Court, SW5
Model Engineer Exhibition
– Wembley Conference Centre, Wembley

February
Crufts Dog Show
– Earls Court, SW5
International Canoe Exhibition
– Crystal Palace Sports Centre, SE19

March
(or April)
Easter Parade
– Battersea Park, SW11
(or April)
Harness Horse Parade
– Regents Park, NW1
(or April)
International Model Railway Exhibition
– Royal Horticultural Society Halls, SW1
(or April)
Oxford v Cambridge University Boat Race
– Putney to Mortlake
Stampex
– Royal Horticultural Society Halls, SW1
Sailboat – RYA Dinghy Exhibition
– Crystal Palace Sports Centre, SE19

April
Carlsberg Round London Boat Marathon
– Putney Hard to Little Venice to
   Putney Hard

May
Covent Garden Punch & Judy Festival
– St. Paul's Church, WC2
Historic Commercial Vehicle Run
– Battersea Park to Brighton

June
Beating Retreat
– Horse Guards Parade, SW1
Biggin Hill Air Fair
– Biggin Hill, Kent
Covent Garden Children's Festival
– Covent Garden, WC2
Trooping the Colour
– Horse Guards Parade, SW1
Wimbledon Lawn Tennis Championships
– All England Club, SW19

July
(or August)
Children's Books of the Year Exhibition
– Barbican Centre, EC2 and Royal Festival
   Hall, SE1
National Festival of Music for Youth
– South Bank Concert Halls, SE1
Royal Tournament
– Earls Court, SW5
Street Entertainers Festival
– Covent Garden, WC2

August
Children's Day
– South Bank, SE1
London Riding Horse Parade
– Rotten Row, Hyde Park, W2
Notting Hill Carnival Children's Day
– Notting Hill, W10

September
Autumn Stampex/BPE
– Royal Horticultural Society Halls, SW1
Clown Convention
– Covent Garden, WC2
Thamesday
– South Bank Centre, SE1

October
Games Day
– Royal Horticultural Society Halls, SW1
Horse of the Year Show
– Wembley Arena, Wembley
Punch & Judy Fellowship Festival
– Covent Garden Piazza, WC2

November
Caravan Camping Holiday Show
– Earls Court, SW5
Fireworks Display
– Alexandra Park, Wood Green, N22
Lord Mayor's Show
– City of London
RAC Veteran Car Run
– Hyde Park Corner to Brighton

December
National Cat Club Show
– Olympia, W14
Olympia International Showjumping
– Olympia, W14
Royal Smithfield Show
– Earls Court, SW5

For precise dates concerning these events, contact your nearest major Tourist Information Centre or the London Tourist Board direct on 01-730 3488.

Remember, parking in central London can be difficult. Very few attractions have their own car park so for your convenience we have listed the nearest National Car Parks.

Some car parks near places of interest. This is not a complete list. Opening hours and prices vary. Please check with the relevant garage.

a NCP London Wall, EC2
Tel: 01-628 7468

b NCP Tower Hill,
Lower Thames Street, EC3
Tel: 01-626 2082.

c NCP Paternoster,
(Ave Maria Lane), EC4
Tel: 01-248 7527

d NCP Snowfields, SE1
Tel: 01-407 1053

e NCP Marylebone Road, NW1
Tel: 01-935 6078

f East Heath Road, Hampstead, NW3

g NCP YMCA Tottenham Court Road, W1
Tel: 01-636 6593

h NCP Burlington Garage,
Old Burlington Street, W1
Tel: 01-437 2313

i NCP Brewer Street, W1
Tel: 01-734 7339

j NCP Park Lane, W1
Tel: 01-262 1814

k NCP Upper St. Martin's Lane, WC2
Tel: 01-836 7451

l NCP Drury Lane,
Covent Garden, WC2
Tel: 01-242 7577

m NCP Swiss Centre,
Leicester Street, W1
Tel: 01-734 1032

n NCP Brunswick Square, WC1
Tel: 01-278 9792

o NCP Dolphin Square Garage,
Grosvenor Road, SW1
Tel: 01-834 1077

p NCP Abingdon Street, SW1
Tel: 01-222 8621

q NCP Arlington House,
Arlington Street, SW1
Tel: 01-499 3312

r NCP Semley Place,
Buckingham Palace Road, SW1
Tel: 01-730 7905

t NCP Young Street, W8
Tel: 01-937 7420

u Travelwise Garage,
244 Brompton Road, SW3
Tel: 01-589 9815

v NCP Bayswater Road, W8
Tel: 01-229 9381

w NCP Arthur Court (Queensway)
Tel: 01-221 2906

x NCP Colonnades (Porchester Terrace)
Tel: 01-221 8020

y NCP Vauxhall Bridge Foot, SW8
Tel: 01-735 3964

z Park Row, Greenwich, SE10

aa Burnley Street, Greenwich, SE10
(Access via Stockwell Street)

bb Cutty Sark Gardens, Greenwich, SE10
Coaches only. Max time 90 mins.
Limited car parking underground

cc Blackheath Avenue,
Greenwich Park, SE10

SUBJECT INDEX